Gender and Class in the Egyptian Women's Movement,

1925–1939

Middle East Studies Beyond Dominant Paradigms

Peter Gran, *Series Editor*

Gender and Class

in the Egyptian Women's Movement, 1925–1939

Changing Perspectives

CATHLYN MARISCOTTI

Syracuse University Press

First Edition 2008
08 09 10 11 12 13   6 5 4 3 2 1

The paper used in this publication meets the minimum requirements of
American National Standard for Information Sciences—Permanence of
Paper for Printed Library Materials, ANSI Z39.48–1984.∞™

For a listing of books published and distributed by Syracuse University Press,
visit our Web site at SyracuseUniversityPress.syr.edu

ISBN-13: 978-0-8156-3170-5   ISBN-10: 0-8156-3170-7

Library of Congress Cataloging-in-Publication Data
Mariscotti, Cathlyn.
Gender and class in the Egyptian women's movement, 1925–1939 :
changing perspectives / Cathlyn Mariscotti. — 1st ed.
p. cm.
Includes bibliographical references and index.
ISBN 978-0-8156-3170-5 (hardcover : alk. paper)
1. Feminism—Egypt.   2. Feminism and literature—Egypt.
3. Women's rights—Egypt.   4. Women in development—Egypt.
I. Title.
HQ1793.M388 2008
305.420962'09042—dc22
2008027916

Manufactured in the United States of America

In appreciation for my mother's lifelong support,
I dedicate this book to her.

CATHLYN MARISCOTTI is an associate professor of history at Holy Family University in Philadelphia, Pennsylvania.

Contents

Foreword

PETER GRAN

Books in the series Middle East Studies Beyond Dominant Paradigms are intended to explore and challenge aspects of the dominant paradigm in the field of history. Cathlyn Mariscotti's work successfully achieves this goal. In her carefully researched monograph, she examines the formative period of institutional feminism in Egypt and concludes that upper-class women who were feminists used their class position to try to control feminist women from the lower middle class on a broad range of issues—an effort that the latter resisted. Mariscotti presents protagonists for each point of view: the well-known Huda Sha'rawi for the upper-class position, and Munira Thabit and Fatima Yusuf representing that of the lower middle class. The character of feminism in Egypt was shaped by this class struggle.

Mariscotti's originality lies not only in her reinterpretation of these iconic personalities but also in her presentation of a generically important issue in feminist writing—one not seen in a long time: the issue of class conflict among women, feminists at that. For the longest time, women have been marginal to the discourse on class. Studies of feminism have been assumed the unity of women without probing the nature and limitations of that unity. Many works in recent years employ the term *feminisms,* or the phrase *women and class,* but it is difficult to find a work in the wider literature on women's studies, much less the narrower field of Egyptian women's studies, where class conflict is recognized as underlying the competition of feminisms, dividing a movement otherwise unified. The field of Middle East women's studies uses either a top-down approach, with the

ix

West as a model, or a multiculturalist approach, exploring a certain pluralizing of elites around culture. Mariscotti's work succeeds in challenging both these perspectives. Hers is the first work, to my knowledge, to base itself on the indigenous dynamic as opposed to simply the indigenous.

Acknowledgments

This book is an outgrowth of my dissertation that was completed in 1994. It has been a long time in the making. I would like to thank the American Research Center in Egypt (ARCE) for helping me secure a fellowship from the United States Information Agency to do research in Egypt in 1989–90. The people at ARCE then and when I returned in 2005 were most gracious. I have long wished to thank the librarians at the Dar al-Kutub for their assistance. Lamia El-Behary, whom I met in the Dar al-Kutub, assisted me in navigating the Dawriyat. I will always remember her kindness. Completion of this work was supported by a Taylor Grant from Holy Family University.

In the early stages, Mervat Hatem, Kathy Uno, and Tom Patterson provided both theoretical and substantive guidance to the development of this work. As always, my sincerest gratitude goes to my mentor, Peter Gran, for sharing his belief that there is always more to history, and we must keep searching. I would also like to thank Peter for his unwavering support of my efforts throughout my academic career. More recently, Bob Vitalis and Hoda Elsadda met with me to discuss aspects of this work. I am grateful for their time.

Among the other people that I must acknowledge is my friend and colleague Millie Savard, who provided assistance with the theoretical and comparative works on Latin America. Debby Kramer, the Interlibrary Loan librarian at Holy Family University, found all of the materials that I needed to complete the work. My students, especially José Mayan and Celeste Thompson, helped me hone the theoretical development of this work through our discussions in class. I must acknowledge the support of my extended family, whose members assisted in a variety of ways. Special gratitude is reserved for my husband, Mark, and my son, Philip, who had to endure my absence while I worked on this book. The anonymous readers provided excellent comments for revision. Finally, thank you to the editors and staff at Syracuse University Press for facilitating this publication.

Gender and Class in the Egyptian Women's Movement,

1925–1939

1

Egyptian Women and the Early Feminist Movement

Introduction and Overview of the Literature

Although many excellent examples exist of substantive research on the history of Egyptian women in the early twentieth century, the search for a workable framework of analysis has not kept pace with the amount of information produced on the subject. This lack of theory in the study of Egyptian women's history has led scholars to fall back on the older Orientalist paradigm[1] or its positivist successor, neo-Orientalism, in their efforts to organize this substantive material. The older Orientalism framed Egyptian women's experience primarily in ethnic and religious contexts. For Orientalists, Egyptian women's Arab ethnicity and Islamic religion confined them to the nonpublic, ahistorical realm of the family. Only through an acceptance of Western reform, including Western bourgeois feminism, could Egyptian women achieve historicity. Neo-Orientalism has contributed to this problem by focusing on other political and social structures in a positivist manner, producing genealogies of

---

1. See Said 1979 for a discussion of the Western creation and maintenance of the discourse of Orientalism as a reified epistemological construct of the Middle East in the Western historical tradition. Though Said attempted to challenge this paradigm, much of the scholarship on the Middle East remains constructed within this framework. While the quantity of substantive research has increased on the subject of Egyptian women and is quite useful, my contention is that the theoretical framework needs to be broadened in order to address questions not raised by the dominant paradigm.

structures to which women are marginally related. The problem with Orientalism and, by extension, the neo-Orientalist perspective is that the field has not moved much further theoretically from its Eurocentric positivist and hermeneutic origins. Thus the old dichotomies remain with respect to the public/private debate, the application of separate perspectives for the study of Western and Egyptian history, and the acceptance of Egypt's current position in the undeveloped world as timeless, thereby maintaining a polarity with the West. This methodological framework favors the activities of Egyptian women who worked within these Western-constructed dichotomies during the interwar period. They could then provide this history to the rest of Egyptian women.

The problem with the current paradigm is that it assumes that Egyptian history can be understood only relationally to the West. Any dynamic occurring *within* Egypt during this period that cannot be comprehended in Western terms is either considered aberrant or is ignored. Thus, Orientalist and neo-Orientalist scholarship views disparagingly Islamic fundamentalist, fascist, or Marxist challenges to the liberal nationalist state, and makes no attempt to integrate these movements into a historical perspective.[2] Each movement is considered on its own terms because the movements appear unrelated. However, the fact that the movements, despite their varying perspectives, appeared at the same time suggests that they represented forms of popular opposition to the liberal nationalist state in the 1920s and 1930s. By focusing on the conflict, a picture of what was going on in Egypt may emerge. Such an analysis would not benefit the positivist cause, however, as it would have to consider responses from the lower classes in civil society and the underclass and would necessarily delay the linear trajectory of the history of the dominant paradigm. With the increase of substantive research on the history of Egyptian women in the early twentieth century, new frameworks of analysis become possible.

2. See Badran 1991 for a discussion of the limitations of Islam and Islamic feminist organizations in Egypt for creating radical changes in gender relations. Badran insists that only secular feminists can initiate this change. Her work, however, remains the best source for substantive information on the Egyptian women's movement and the lives of Huda Sha'rawi, Nabawiya Musa, and Ceza Nabarawi.

Even though Nikki Keddie called for a de-Orientalization of Middle Eastern women's history in 1979, Orientalism is still evident in studies on the history of Middle Eastern and, more specifically, Egyptian women.[3] One example of this perspective is the concept that upper-class Egyptian women were more in need of liberation than their lower-class counterparts owing to the fact that the upper class were secluded and veiled.[4] This analysis rests solely on the concept that liberation for women implies access to public space, a decidedly Western bourgeois feminist concept. Another example can be found in the connection between Muslim reformism and ruling-class feminism in Egypt in the late nineteenth and early twentieth centuries (Jayawardena 1986, 48–50). Some scholars trace the beginning of this modernist and reformist trend to the reign of Muhammad 'Ali and acknowledge an acceleration of reform and modernization in Egypt under Khedive Isma'il.[5] With regard to Muslim reformism, Jamal al-Din al-Afghani and, later, Muhammad 'Abduh sought to promote a separation of religion and politics in Islam and a reliance on Western science and technology. Both al-Afghani and 'Abduh were staunch supporters of limited education for women. In the literature on the subject, 'Abduh's disciple Qasim Amin emerged as the champion for women's rights in Egypt after the 1899 publication of his book *Tahrir al-Mar'a*.

3. Useful sources that can be employed to treat Middle Eastern women in a differentiated manner can be found in Keddie 1979, Malti-Douglas 1991, Posusney 1991, and Ahmed 1992.

4. See Marsot 1978 (270) for an example of this type of framework. A newer example of top-down analysis with respect to Muslim women includes Talhami 1996. Also see the new narrative of the women's movement in Al-Ali 2000. For a more unique and indigenous approach, though still within the dominant paradigm, see Sonbol 2000. Sonbol discusses the role of Huda Sha'rawi as a representative of elite women who set a standard of modernity against women of the *'amma*. She does not, however, show differentiation among (mass) women or ways that they challenged the standards set by Sha'rawi and women of the *khassa* or elite.

5. See Hourani 1983 for the treatment of the influence of secular reform in Islam and its relationship to the development of liberal Arab nationalism. Also see Vatikiotis 1991 for a discussion of how state-making under Muhammad 'Ali, coupled with Islamic reform, was progressive for all Egyptians.

As the ruling-class women's movement became tied to Western constructs that included the supremacy of Western technology and science
and the concept of the separation of church and state, it seemed logical
that these women were worthy of historical treatment and would be capable of bringing history to Egyptian women as a whole. Although 'Abduh
and Amin advocated education for women in order to make them better
wives and mothers, they also supported women's entrance into public
space. The suggestion that harem women's lack of access to public space
was the greatest obstacle Egyptian females had to overcome is narrow
given that lower-class women were not veiled or confined to a harem.
Furthermore, to argue that Egyptian women, especially from the ruling
class, needed to enter public space in order to become historical figures
negates the importance of activities they performed within the structure
of the family.

This paradigm is an outgrowth of the public/private debate, grounded
in both Liberal Enlightenment and cultural feminism, and espoused by
middle-class women in the West during the eighteenth and nineteenth
centuries. Both of these feminist perspectives acknowledged the existence
of separate spheres for men and women: the public, productive, and historical sphere of men, and the private, reproductive, nonhistorical sphere
of women, apparent even in public space. This analysis is grounded in the
Western view that acknowledges the existence of real dichotomies, notably the separation of public and private spheres, of church and state, and of
science and religion.[6] The problem with feminist theory has been to con-
flate public/private spheres with public/private space. If Egyptian women
were confined to a harem, they must not have had access to the public
sphere. It is difficult, however, to defend the idea that elite women's lack of
access to public *space* was a major source of their oppression. In *Women
in Nineteenth Century Egypt,* Judith Tucker has shown that elite women
acted as *multazimat* (tax farmers) at a time when *iltizam* (tax farms) were
virtually private property. With these assets, elite women endowed and
administered *awqaf* (philanthropic endowments), establishing hospitals,

6. For examples of works within this genre, see Marsot 1978 (269), Philipp 1978 (279),
and Jayawardena 1986 (48–50).

mosques, and other social institutions, which they employed as tax shelters before the twentieth century (1985, 93–96). Thus, even at home, elite Egyptian women were continually engaged in public economic activities.

Organizing Egyptian women's history within the nationalist framework replicates the Western paradigm again.[7] The nationalist movement incorporated Western liberal traditions such as the concept of individuality, constitutionalism, and education (Philipp 1978, 285; Badran 1995, 74–88). By framing history in such a manner, the West became the great savior that provided the opportunity for true history within the confines of its historical tradition. Any internal dynamic within Egypt at this period that may have involved other classes or indigenous historical traditions is simply ignored. Institutional feminism in Egypt inevitably became the historical experience for all Egyptian women.

Lacking a framework that acknowledges the indigenous economic or political situation in Egypt in the early twentieth century, ruling-class women's history is one where they alone are seen as suffering from the dual form of oppression of British colonialism and patriarchy (Badran 1988, 30). According to this analysis, lower-class Egyptian women who had access to public space apparently were not affected by patriarchy in the same way as harem women. Patriarchy, in this framework, is tied to British colonialism. Harem women were more oppressed by patriarchy because they did not have access to the public sphere by virtue of the fact that they did not have access to public space. As a result, elite women bore the burden of colonialism and patriarchy more than the lower class; they had to ally themselves to the nationalist cause and Western bourgeois feminism in order to defeat both the British and the men of their own class. With this line of argument, however, questions arise as to what happened after the British left Egypt and the ruling class became the new dominant power. Were ruling-class women finally freed from patriarchy? Were lower-class

7. See Baron 2005, where she organizes Egyptian women around the structure of nationalism, employing textual productions, including photographs and cartoons, to examine Egyptian women's cross-class nationalist political contributions in the early twentieth century. Baron presents Labiba Ahmad as the sole Egyptian Islamic nationalist, divergent more than resistant.

women freed from the dual oppression of colonialism and patriarchy, or did they simply undergo no change since they were not oppressed by patriarchy in the first place? As the history of lower-class women is missing from the discourse or exists only in relation to elite women's history, it is difficult to find answers to these questions.

Was Egyptian institutional feminism, then, the only movement extant at the time that could incorporate all women's needs, or did alternative movements exist that may have been at odds with ruling-class feminism?

The notion that elite feminism superseded class enhances the static and therefore ahistorical quality of this feminism in relation to other Egyptian women. Moreover, the assumption that this feminism was and is the only one capable of freeing Egyptian women from patriarchy presupposes that the relationship of lower-class women to production and politics was similar to that of elite women during this period. Is gender, then, a constant across class lines, allowing one group of women to speak for all the women in the society?

The inability of such an approach to integrate class into a historical analysis of the period sets up a paradigm of ruling-class women providing change to the rest of the females in society, thus replicating the scenario of the West providing change or history to Egypt. The literature on the subject portrays elite women as being in the most favorable position, economically and politically, to bestow Western bourgeois feminism upon all women in Egypt. As a result of elite women's social position and male kin connections, they were better able to effect political change than their lower-class counterparts (Abdel Kader 1987, 92). Such a theory, however, challenges the premise that elite women needed to access public space to affect the public sphere. Another hypothesis is that, given their superior economic position, elite women's ideals would less likely be compromised (92).

While ruling-class women in Egypt possessed the material conditions to launch an effective crusade against patriarchy, the issue that does not seem to be raised in the literature of the dominant paradigm is whether all Egyptian women would benefit equally from elite women's political activities. Without a thorough analysis of the internal dynamic going on in Egypt between 1925 and 1939, the comparative sense of the elite being in a better position to perform these activities is hollow given the possibility that they were only working for their own interests. As such, the current literature makes many assumptions but provides little real historical analysis. The very idea that ruling-class women did not have to work and thus would not have to compromise their ideals for the necessity of earning a living gives a clue that Egyptian women who did not possess this fortune or who desired to work may have had different historical agendas.

Therefore, the perspective lends itself to a view that lower-class women were either simply recipients of the harem women's advancements or were passively waiting to imitate the activities of the elite (Marsot 1978, 270). Apparently, lower-class Egyptian women's ability to imitate the elite provided for a breakdown in the class barriers that separated the country's women (Badran 1986, 137). With such an approach, the nonelite were incapable of any human impulse other than the ability to receive or imitate. Ruling-class women controlled the gates of history and, as such, were credited with a whole range of activities, including respectability for waged work, even though such was not an important issue for them (Marsot 1978, 270).

Where there is an acknowledgment in the scholarship that institutional feminism in Egypt was strictly for ruling-class women, the history of other women's relationship to it is written from the perspective of elite women's philanthropic activities for the benefit of the less fortunate in Egypt (Philipp 1978, 284; Badran 1995, 111–23). However, no analysis is made in the literature on how philanthropy was employed by the elite to assimilate other women into the nationalist movement in Egypt. By organizing history in this manner, a chronological and a generational history emerges that enhances the view that Egyptian ruling-class feminism was the only movement with which Egyptian women became involved during the early twentieth century. In this history, their achievements are picked up and carried further by the next generation, often by those women who had benefited from university education, thus providing a Western positivist view of the history of institutional feminism in Egypt. Indicative of this is Soha Abdel Kader, who moves progressively from the feminist activities of Huda Sha'rawi in the 1920s to the social activism of Suhayr al-Qalamawy in the 1930s.[8] Then in the 1940s, Duria Shafiq emerges to continue the institutional feminist tradition.[9] Some variations of this view are less optimistic. One line argues that feminism in Egypt did not survive into the 1930s with no further explanation (Jayawardena 1986, 55). In each approach, the perspective is on the progress made by elite women, especially Huda Sha'rawi and the Egyptian Feminist Union, and how this progress affected all Egyptian women, not only across class lines but across time lines as well.

In these analyses, only the names and faces seem to change. No attempts are made to uncover challenges to institutional feminism within Egypt that may have caused its decline by the 1930s. Furthermore, the progress of Egyptian women represented by people such as Suhayr al-Qalamawy and Duria Shafiq is credited to the elite who worked to open the universities to Egyptian women. The existence of a group of women already engaged in the professions without university training who may have had different agendas than the harem women and who may have had a larger impact on advancing women into professional areas is rarely mentioned in the literature.[10] Therefore, the majority of the analyses on the subject have focused on a narrow perspective of the history of Egyptian women during this period. The picture presented in much of the literature is one in which institutional feminism was the only activity carried on by Egyptian women of the period, and that this feminism was accepted wholeheartedly by and benefited all Egyptian women.

The seeming sense of the unity of Egyptian elite feminism underscores once again the simplicity of its history in comparison to that of

8. Abdel Kader jumps neatly from the elite feminism of Huda Sha'rawi in the 1920s to the social-activist feminism of Suhayr al-Qalamawy in the 1930s without analyzing how this transition took place. See Badran 1995 for a similar study that covers issues relating to elite Egyptian feminism over a period of a century, highlighting collusion among Egyptian women and little, if any, conflict.

9. Nelson (1996) provides a similar analysis as Abdel Kader though it is Duria Shafiq who inherits the Sha'rawi legacy in 1940.

10. Malik Hifni Nasif, Nabawiya Musa, Munira Thabit, Labiba Ahmad, Fatima, al-Yusuf, Ruza Antun Haddad, Fatima Rushdi, and others were early role models for Egyptian managerial-class women.

the West. It also lends itself to further comparisons with feminist movements in other Middle Eastern countries under the continual Orientalist banner of ethnicity—in most cases, Arab—and religion, always Islam.[11] The organization of Egyptian women's history in this manner maintains the polarity between the Middle East and the West, strengthening the Western theoretical dichotomization mentioned earlier. Since all women in society are dependent on the elite for history, then ethnicity and religion become the means for organizing studies of nonelite women. With regard to ethnicity, symbolic anthropological approaches to the study of Egyptian nonelite women result in confining lower-class women within a reified culture that gives them meaning, effectively removing them from any subjective interaction with even their own culture.[12] Therefore, nonelite women only receive a cultural framework, one that symbolic anthropologists, among others, view as static, leaving them at the mercy of elite women's history.

Religion, specifically Islam, as it applies to Egyptian women, receives a similar theoretical treatment. Thus, the debate rages as to whether Islam is bad or good for women and feminism (Ahmed 1982, 161).[13] No attempts

11. Baron 2005 provides for a broadening of ethnic and religious structures to include Copts, Sudanese, Bedouins, and Syrians (Levantines) but still maintains the ethnic and religious structural framework.

12. See Abu-Lughod 1986 and 1993 for a symbolic anthropological approach to the study of Bedouin women in Egypt. Similarly, Boddy 1989 takes a symbolic anthropological approach to the *zar* ritual in Sudan, a ritual prevalent in Egypt as well. Boddy states that the *zar* gives meaning to Sudanese women, reifying the ritual as an object that Sudanese women do not subjectively control. For an alternative view on the practice of the *zar* in Egypt, see Mayers 1984, who argues that peasant women in Egypt subjectively began to employ it from Sudan at the turn of the twentieth century as a means of resistance to the dispossession of their land, which resulted in their forced migration and urbanization.

13. See also Mernissi 1988 (8–9), who views veiling in the contemporary Middle East as a struggle between lower-middle-class fundamentalist men and secular Muslim women of the upper-middle class. Mernissi fails to acknowledge lower-middle-class women's subjective decision to wear the veil and their contribution to its styling. MacLeod 1991 attempts to put contemporary Egyptian Muslim women's protest into historical perspective, though she does not analyze what the hegemonic culture is that they are opposing.

are made to see how Islam differs from class to class, or among different ethnicities, or within the same sex, or between the two sexes. In this perspective, Islam becomes a unified religion that is practiced in the same manner by all Muslims in the world and therefore can be equally applied in a theoretical analysis of the history of Muslim women.[14] Thus, scholars who work within the dominant paradigm reify the present form of social structures, religion, and ethnicity, and attempt to place the present form of the structures into the past.

Employing this perspective, there is no need to analyze changes in the social structures over time; there have been none. Religion and ethnicity now become static mechanisms that affect people rather than the other way around. This may explain why few analyses have been presented to examine how women in the past may have reordered their ethnic and religious identification in terms of nationalism, unionism, Marxism, communism, fascism, Islamic fundamentalism, or any one of a variety of cultural organizations tied to economic and political concerns. Another example of this Orientalist reductionism with respect to cultural structures includes the use of race and racial discrimination, where race replaces ethnicity and religion as the mechanism in history.[15]

In these studies, cultural structures become detached from political and economic ones, placing the Middle East, and more specifically Egypt, in a discursive cultural realm outside of the broader global political economy. This detachment leads to an inability on the part of scholars to view the fluidity of social structures such as gender, family, ethnicity, and religion with respect to changing political and economic situations. Egyptian women become trapped in unchanging social structures that make them appear to possess a different framework of history than Western women. Non-Western feminists have pointed out the problems Western feminists face when examining the history of non-Western women. "Feminist scholars have a

14. See Kandiyoti 1987 (317–38) for an example of this type of analysis.

15. See Powell 2003 for an example of the use of race in understanding the history of Egyptian nationalism. Baron 2005 employs Powell in her analysis of Egyptian nationalism. Race has become a new structural framework, along with ethnicity and religion, within which to study the history of the Middle East.

tendency to proceed by reversal: non-Western women are what we are not. These tendencies of projection and reversal situate non-Western women in a subordinate position within feminist theoretical and textual productions. These self-validating exercises affirm our feminist subjectivity while denying those of non-Western women" (Ong 1988, 79–93). Thus, it is important to attempt to reduce the level of objectification when analyzing the history of non-Western women. The failure of some feminist scholars in the field of Middle Eastern studies to accomplish this task has only served to enhance the power of Orientalism as a whole.

A neo-Orientalist approach that traces the coming of feminism from the West to Egypt through the American missionary schools in Beirut, especially the Syrian Protestant College, situates the locus of the women's awakening in Alexandria, not in Cairo (Booth 2001).[16] The presence of feminists such as Zaynab Fawwaz in Alexandria does not necessarily place the locus of the women's struggle or the development of institutional feminism in Alexandria. Without a contextualization of these women in the wider social dynamic of the period, their contribution to the evolution of Egyptian feminism is tenuous at best. In fact, of the twenty-seven "women's" journals published between the late nineteenth century and 1957 that are listed in Irene Fenoglio-Abd El Aal's book, *Defense et illustration de L'Egyptienne,* only two of the journals were published in Alexandria (1988, 18–19). Fenoglio-Abd El Aal goes on to state that in the early twentieth century, Cairo was the most representative of Egyptian cultural activity, especially with respect to women's culture (1988, 19). Though Syrian Christians played an influential role in the professions at the beginning of the twentieth century, Egyptians increasingly replaced them in the fields of journalism, theater, medicine, and law after the 1919 revolution (Landau 1958). The Egyptianization of the professions would have had, in any case, a profound impact on the Western connection, via Beirut and Alexandria, if one existed in the first place. This shift from the influence of Levantines in Alexandria to Egyptians in Cairo changed the locus of the struggle to a strictly internal one. This change needs to be acknowledged in the theoretical treatment of the period and its subjects.

16. Baron 1994 begins this approach and Booth 2001 continues it.

In these examples, some Western scholars, feminists included, continue to employ the older Orientalism and neo-Orientalism to maintain the theoretical polarity between the West and the Middle East, thus ignoring internal dynamic in the region in favor of highlighting a history that begins with the coming of the West and Western institutions. In order to reconstruct the history of Middle Eastern women, including those from Egypt, it is necessary to dissolve this dichotomy by first examining how the West and the Middle East interact with each other with respect to politics and economics and to explore in what specific ways women are linked to this relationship.

For Egyptian women in the interwar period, such an examination would place ruling-class women and their institutional feminism within the broader economic and political climate in Egypt rather than connecting them only to the nationalist movement. It also would consider challenges to ruling-class women from other Egyptian women.

This approach can include an analysis of Egypt's marginal position with respect to the world economy and how this historical situation helped to shape the country's political and economic development. The developmentalist's perspective can be useful, but it must remain devoid of Orientalist influences. In "Pride, Purdah, or Paychecks: What Maintains the Gender Division of Labor in Rural Egypt?" James Toth cites that gender division of labor in Egypt is easy to maintain; it is the only division in the society employers can exploit given that Egypt lacks the racial and ethnic divisions found in the United States (1991, 223).[17] While Toth makes a contribution to understanding the gender division of labor and its effects on Egyptian women, he does so at the expense of maintaining a theoretical division between the West and Egypt.

17. See also Brink 1991, who posits that Egyptian male outmigration to the oil-producing countries in the Middle East is progressive for Egyptian women, as the money generated from such migration allows Egyptian wives to live separately from their mothers-in-law. In Brink's analysis, it is not poverty that oppresses Egyptian women as much as it is the dominance of the mother-in-law in the unchanging Egyptian family. For Brink, Egyptian women's liberation lies in changing the family structure from an extended to a nuclear or subnuclear female head of the household family, similar to the family structure that has become more common in the West.

According to Toth's analysis, Egypt is more socially homogenous than the United States and less complex. He also argues that the United States does not have the problem of gender division of labor because it lacks *purdah* and female docility. In line with these assertions, Toth attempts to analyze women's subordinate position in the labor market and how Egypt's integration into it affects women's socioeconomic position. However, by doing it in this manner, he reinforces the Orientalist perspective that Egypt is a simple society. This view assumes that Egypt cannot be treated in a methodologically similar way to the United States even though Egypt is quite diverse socially and gender division of labor does exist in the United States as well as in Egypt. An approach capable of bridging this theoretical gap between Western and Middle Eastern women would aid an analysis of the history of Egyptian women and the Middle East as a whole.

Part of this process of dissolving dichotomies to provide a more differentiated framework must include the concept of class.

> In discussing ideologies regarding women, as in other issues, a consideration of class is vital—not necessarily the class origin of the individual who puts forth specific ideas, but rather what class groups he or she appeals to and represents. This has scarcely been discussed in relation to ideologies regarding women, and yet if these are studied attentively, the class appeal of the holders of different views is usually clear. In Egypt, both the earliest advocates of the liberation of women, like Muhammad 'Abduh and Qasim Amin, and their more thoroughgoing pre–World War II male and female followers tended to belong, or at least to appeal, to an upper- or upper-middle-class group with ties to the British, who were moderate in their politics both toward the British and on local issues. Egypt's more radical anti-imperialists, beginning with Mustafa Kamil and continuing through the Muslim Brotherhood, were both more petty bourgeois and popular in their appeal and more defensive of traditional ways, including traditional law and status regarding women. The application of class analysis of ideologies and movements on more than a crude simplistic level is rare for the Middle East and virtually non-existent in the study of attitudes toward women and women's activities. (Keddie 1979, 234–35)

A class analysis of the history of Egyptian women in the early twentieth century could reveal more closely the connections between the ruling class and the West and Western institutions and lower-class challenges to those connections.

The application of class analysis must be consistent with the way it is employed in Western contexts. Otherwise, the result is an Orientalist Marxism in which political economy takes a back seat to the primacy of ethnicity and religion in an analysis of the history of Middle Eastern women.[18] In addition to class analysis, the concept of gender must be reevaluated to include its relationship to a particular hegemony. Women's relationship to men and patriarchy differs from class to class and from developed areas to underdeveloped areas in the world. By viewing gender in this manner, gender does not remain unchanging while economic and political climates change but necessarily becomes part of that change.

This reconstruction is not to be construed as an outright rejection of bourgeois feminism but as a broadening of the concepts of gender and how women in various relationships to the economy and politics experience different levels of oppression and respond to it. Maria Mies explains:

> Without a radical feminist critique of the middle class ideal of womanhood—with its specific national and cultural manifestations—there is the danger that middle-class women, even if they are genuinely committed to women's liberation and to the liberation of all oppressed and exploited, will remain blind to the truly progressive and human elements to be found among the so-called "backward" classes and communities with regard to women. (1986, 209)

Specifically, with regard to ruling-class women and institutional feminism in Egypt, the importance of debates involving changes in the Muslim personal status laws would be reevaluated given the fact that such

---

18. See Ghoussoub 1987 for an example of this Orientalist Marxist perspective. For a deconstruction of Ghoussoub's perspective see Hammami and Rieker 1988. Some of the best feminist writing on the Middle East discusses Western ideas about the area and not the area itself. See, for example, Kabbani 1986 and 1994.

issues themselves had undergone changes from the Ottoman period to the twentieth century. Amira Sonbol has shown that multiple interpretations of *Shari'a* with respect to the minimum age for marriage and minority status of children were extant in Egypt during the Ottoman period and that these interpretations became uniform and state sponsored, controlled by the new hegemonic elites, with the creation of the Egyptian state (1996, 36). While Sonbol does not judge whether the new laws benefited women and children, she does suggest that it limited their autonomy until the age of twenty-one. Another possibility is that many of the issues related to the personal status laws, such as polygamy and a man's sole right to divorce, may not have been as important to women of the lower classes. Lower-class men would have found it difficult to support more than one wife, for example, while ruling-class women stood to lose more from divorce, materially, than did lower-class women, who were more than likely already engaged in waged work, formally or informally. Analyses of this type exist with regard to studies on Western women and need to be applied when studying Middle Eastern women.[19] Then the oppression of elite women and the resistance to their own oppression would not continue to be the hallmark of history for all of the women in the society.

When examining the history of elite Egyptian women and their institutional feminism, it is necessary to reevaluate its progressiveness in relation to nationalism and to study more closely the connection between nationalism and ethnicity and religion. In that way, social structures such as family, ethnicity, nationalism, and religion are placed within their historical context and do not remain static outside of history. Thomas C. Patterson, in "Tribes, Chiefdoms, and Kingdoms in the Inca Empire," has traced the rise of the Inca imperial state in the fifteenth century to a tribute-based economy and has noted a concurrent rise of nationalism that proved ethnocidal to peripheral peoples, forcing them to reconstruct new ethnicities in order to resist the growing nationalism of the Inca (1987, 117–25). Patterson's work shows the fluidity of ethnicity

19. Walkowitz 1980 discusses the different perspectives of gender and sexuality held by ruling-class and working-class women in Victorian England and examines the role of ruling-class women and the state in reshaping the discourse of gender and sexuality.

with regard to political and economic conditions; he avoids the Orientalist trap by providing the analysis within a pre-Western and preglobal capitalist context.

A similar analysis could be applied to the study of ruling-class women and their employment of an institutional feminism in the creation and maintenance of the Egyptian state. Such an analysis would not accept a priori the concept that state-making and nationalism, of any variety and at any time during Egypt's long history, were necessarily progressive for all Egyptians. Movements associated with these concepts would have constituted one aspect of gender or ethnicity or religion that would have proven ethnocidal for marginalized women of the lower classes or for peripheralized groups such as Copts, Bedouins, Nubians, Jews, Greeks, Italians, and Armenians, to name a few. Women of these marginalized groups in Egypt may have formed new ethnicities, religions, or forms of established religions and organized within these structures to resist, on some level, nationalism and institutional feminism in the early twentieth century. Instead of the Orientalist view of static social structures moving across class, across nations, and across time, what is needed is a perspective of what is going on historically at a particular period of time in Egypt. This type of framework could help to explain the decline of institutional feminism by the 1930s, the rise of extraparliamentary organizations in Egypt in the same period, and nonelite women's relationship to these organizations, including their own constructs of themselves as women.

Specifically, with regard to Egypt, several works have been published that have, to one degree or another, successfully attempted to tackle these methodological problems and can be employed in an analysis on Egyptian ruling-class feminism. Both Judith Tucker, in *Women in Nineteenth Century Egypt,* and Judith Gran, in "Impact of the World Market on Egyptian Women," examine Egypt's economic position within the global capitalist economy and its effects on its women (Tucker 1985; Gran 1977, 3–5). Class is a component of each analysis, and the relationship of Egyptian women to their class within the global economy provides a changing view of Egyptian women's history as opposed to a static approach. In "Feminism, Class, and Islam in Turn-of-the-Century Egypt," Juan Ricardo Cole gives a similar perspective specifically with respect to feminism at this period (1981, 388–89). Cole's contribution, drawing on Nada Tomiche, includes viewing the rise of upper-class feminism as a means of resisting modern, Western values such as the increased seclusion of women in the nineteenth century (1981, 390–91).[20] In this way, Cole moves away from the concept that feminism was borrowed from the West to change existing traditional institutions perceived as oppressive to Egyptian women. Such an approach highlights the internal dynamic within Egyptian history, maintaining the focus on Egypt and not the West, and eliminates the methodological dichotomies so favored by Orientalists.

Other scholars have also begun to question the positivist view of nationalism with regard to Egyptian feminism. Mervat Hatem has shown how traditional mechanisms of gender control were employed by Egyptian nationalists to maintain women at home while affording them access to public space (1988, 412–13). On another level, in her article entitled "Arab Culture and Writing Women's Bodies," Leila Ahmed has attempted to provide an integrated, if not class, analysis of Nawal El Saadawi and Alifa Rifaat, two contemporary Egyptian feminist writers (1989, 41–42). Instead of simply including both women in an anthology of Arab feminist writers without any further identification, Ahmed analyzes El Saadawi's Western, middle-class, feminist approach to the writing of Egyptian women's bodies as opposed to Alifa Rifaat's more traditional, Egyptian method. Thus, Ahmed begins to reveal the complexity of feminism in the Arab world and, more specifically, in Egypt. She realizes that Arab and Egyptian women are worthy of the same level of analyses that scholars in the West accord Western women.

Amal al-Subki's book *Al-Haraka al-Nisa'iya fi Misr ma bayn al-Thawratayn 1919 wa 1952* also provides for a more integrated approach

---

20. Cole's analysis is similar to that of Tucker 1985. Both link the fortunes of upper-class women in nineteenth-century Egypt to the decline of the autonomy of the family. Cole also employs Tomiche 1968 (177), who suggests that the family was becoming more conservative as a resistance to modernization. Though Cole's approach is problematic because he continues to view Egyptian women in relation to the family, at least he makes the attempt to shift the focus from the West to the internal dynamic in Egypt.

to the women's movement in Egypt. Although al-Subki does not attempt a great deal of analysis, she documents a broad range of activities in which Egyptian women of many classes were engaged, including waged work. She also juxtaposes the political perspectives of Huda Sha'rawi with women such as Fatima al-Yusuf with regard to political events, including the Anglo-Egyptian Treaty of 1936 (al-Subki 1986). This more complete picture of the variety of views from women of different classes lends a degree of complexity to the history of Egyptian women that is akin to the complexity of the history of women in the West.

Following this framework, *Gender and Class in the Egyptian Women's Movement* seeks to provide a historical analysis of ruling-class and managerial-class Egyptian women's activities during the interwar period. Where other works have relied extensively on archival sources and court records to support narratives and biographies, this work does not seek to offer new data on the subject but to produce a historical argument, a framework within which to examine the complexities of ruling- and managerial-class Egyptian women's struggles over issues crucial to women during this period in Egyptian history. The triumph of modernity (positivism) and its logical, mechanistic, chronological, and spatial successor, postmodernism, have relegated history and its influence on events to a discursive periphery, and rendered the historian suspect in analyzing events.[21] One present conceptualization, globalism, claims that the past has nothing to do with the present, a view that reduces Egyptian women's past contributions to the development of contemporary Egypt to irrelevancy. Postcolonialism (postmodernism) is no better as it eliminates

---

21. Abou-El-Haj 2000 challenges four schools of thought that emerged in the wake of Said's deconstruction of the field. Abou-El-Haj notes that history has suffered in the wake of scholarship that employs theory without primary sources; theory that does not allow the primary sources to take the theory in new directions; the continuance of hermeneutic and religious approaches to the field of West Asian and North African studies (Orientalists and neo-Orientalists who only let the primary texts do the talking); and, finally, postmodernists who employ all sorts of culture taken outside of any other social context (i.e., political, economic) to explain social change. A work of historical argument would avoid any one of these approaches and attempt a synthesis of theory and facts with the understanding that such a synthesis is a process and not an end in itself.

any subjective, human interaction that Egyptian women may have had to essentialist, Eurocentrically constructed mechanisms of time, space, or culture (Dirlik 2000, 28–29).[22]

The older paradigm, derived from Hegel, saw Europe as the final stage of history (modernity) (Dussel 1995, 70–75). This positivist framework acknowledged that all history emanated from the present— Europe, Northern Europe to be precise—to the past—all other areas of the world—effectively denying the non-West the complex dynamic of history and continually recreating the divisions between the West and the rest epistemologically, while ignoring the empirical connections between them (66). European and, now, the United States' democracies and free-market capitalism represent the end, modernity to postmodernity, while everyone else, if they desire freedom and history, must again await the coming of the West for freedom from Oriental Despotism (71). In this conceptualization, people from the rest of the world had nothing to do with Europe's and the United States' modernity or postmodernity, and are therefore not worthy of history or a historical approach.

This willful ignorance of the facts, empiricism, undermines the discourse of history so dependent on essentialism. In short, Eurocentric history is not history at all but heritage, myth. To restore history as a viable discourse, let alone to the Middle East and Egypt, it is necessary to begin with the internal dynamic of the area under study and proceed out, always acknowledging the empirical connections between the West and the rest in the modern and postmodern periods. Scholars' failure to deconstruct Eurocentrism and change their approach has left the non-European, non-Western world in a historical no-man's and no-woman's land capable of being formed any way the West would like. This perspective has resulted in negative ramifications for the discourse of history as a whole. Modernism's linear successor, postmodernism, recreates the same Eurocentric framework (Dussel 1995, 74–75). As such, postmodernism also willfully ignores certain essentialisms, economics and politics, and opts instead for

22. See also Gran 1996 for an example of a recent study that attempts to move beyond Eurocentrism in order to restore a more integrative comparative global historical perspective.

cultural essentialisms that help to define identity but maintain the polarity between Europe/United States and the rest of the world.

With the older Hegelian model or the newer postmodern model, the effect is the same. The line moves forward without challenge to the mechanisms that move the line. People have been effectively removed from having any control over the line or the mechanisms that move it. There exists absolutely no understanding of how the past influenced the present or how people from the non-West had any effect on Europe and the United States. This presentist focused history may well be what has typified European-American history over the past two hundred years and continues with the crisis of historical rationality today in the form of postmodernism (Quijano 1995, 211). If this is the case, then European-American history has been nothing but heritage all along designed not to understand the past but to maintain colonial and postcolonial hegemony. Perhaps history practiced in its purest sense is happening somewhere else in the world, involving less of a rationality reliant on mechanisms and more of an understanding of how the past informs the present, chronologically as well as spatially. A historical treatment, then, of the activities of ruling and managerial-class women in Egypt in the early part of the twentieth century would avoid the European-American modernization/postmodernism approach in order to see the dynamic interplay between these women with respect to economics, politics, culture, and epistemology.

In this vein, women made choices that did not fit a particular rationale but helped to create a rich fabric best understood on its own terms. Acknowledging a complexity of a history not only provides the discourse with renewed meaning but also acts as a counterbalance to the weight of the hegemonic discourse, Eurocentrism. In short, history happens everywhere; this may well be an essentialism in itself that has powerful ramifications for removing epistemological boundaries. Whether the historian works subjectively to interpret history or a postmodernist subjectively creates an epistemological structure and essentializes it, the effect is the same. No mechanism is responsible in either case. This work tries to move beyond the unilinear, mechanistic, Eurocentric approach to expose the dynamic interplay of structures that Egyptian women subjectively chose and transformed in their attempts to advance their agendas and to examine the effect their activities had on Egypt during the interwar period. This work seeks also to avoid taking the concept of nation-state as something like matter, a social structure that can neither be created nor destroyed.

As nation-states are always in the becoming, they are in flux; whether they are important as structures are dependent on the people within the nation-state. Through much of the modern period, elites relied on the nation-state to secure their economic, political, and social control. In the postmodern period, however, the nation-state has become more important to people in the lower echelons of civil society and the under-class who require national bureaucratic institutions, such as the military and police, to gain economic, political, and social status. Members of the elite gain less from the nation-state today and, as a result, their focus tends to be more transnational.[23] Although they must assume an ultranational-ist, patriotic front in order to employ the military and police for their eco-nomic agendas, they do not need the nation-state, per se, to achieve their economic, political, and social goals. Therefore, concepts of the nation-state and nationalism are not static at a given time or over time. With the understanding that the structure of the nation-state is not static, Egyp-tian women in the period under consideration were continually work-ing to craft the fledgling Egyptian nation-state that emerged after 1919. Acknowledging this conceptual fluidity—i.e., that the nation-state is only what its people are contending that it should be at a given time and/or over time—challenges the notion that the state possesses an existence outside of human control.[24]

To examine the dynamic interplay between the ruling class and its creation of an institutional feminism and lower-class women's consent

23. There is a discussion on the development of a transnational managerial ruling class in Hoogvelt 1997. My contention is that while this class fosters cross-national alli-ances, global nonelites are forced to rely on and prop up a nation-state and nationalism in order to gain access to national means of social mobility, including employment in the police and the military.

24. See Di-Capua 2004 (444) for a discussion of the problems associated with Egyp-tian historians' acceptance of the objective existence of the state, leading them to frame their histories in terms of its rise and decline.

and resistance to this feminism, it was necessary to access unique sources that would reflect this exchange between some of the women involved in the struggles and their particular agendas and how their activities were integrated into the wider events of the period. The development of the Egyptian press after the First World War, including a growing number of women's journals, provided a fertile field of information on the issues and the struggles of the interwar period. The nascent Egyptian press became the forum for the national struggles of the period, burgeoning with magazines and newspapers representing a spectrum of classes, political parties, and perspectives, with the possible exception of the Egyptian peasantry. The journals not only reflected the history of the time but attempted to influence that history.

Irene Fenoglio-Abd El Aal states that the twenty-seven women's journals that she documents in her book do not comprise a complete list of the women's journals that were published, and not all of the issues are present given the economic pressure and constraints of the *Dar al-Kutub* to catalogue and maintain the journals in good condition (Fenoglio-Abd El Aal 1988, 18–19). Even acknowledging these limitations with respect to the sources, the periodical section, *Dawriyat*, of al-Hay'a al-Misriya al-'Amma li al-Kitab, the Egyptian National Library, has managed to catalogue and maintain many of the women's journals. Therefore, they seemed a good place to begin the research and, by extension, to employ some of the other sources of the Egyptian general press where women often battled.

The richness and diversity of the women's journals became an archive of sorts to acquire information on the differentiated and complex views on women's issues in Egypt. They also revealed how Egyptian women went about attempting to promote their agendas.[25] The fact that the women themselves were involved in deciding what went into their journals either through their own writings or by editing and owning the journals seemed to reveal most directly their interests. Memoirs, while useful, recollect

25. Soto 1990 (118–20) provides a comparative study on the rise of women's journalism and journalists in Mexico during the 1920s and 1930s. Peter Gran has asserted in his book *Beyond Eurocentrism* (1996) that Egypt is an Italian Road state that can be compared to similar Italian Road states, including Italy, Mexico, and India, in the modern period.

events that have long transpired. I have, however, employed a number of these sources to see how some of the women remembered events of the period. The journals also became a forum for dialogue of sorts about economics, politics, culture, and epistemology, which required choosing a discourse for communication. They revealed the many levels on which the women struggled to be heard. The publications exhibited the complexities of their struggle and the effects it had on Egypt in the twentieth century. Writing in all of these venues also provided an opportunity for the women involved to choose a language, both epistemologically and linguistically, through which they could present their views.

How to approach the journals became the difficult part. Here I allowed the journals and women to speak for themselves. In my research, I discovered that certain women's issues, including education for women, were echoed in many of the journals, while other issues, such as waged work for women or certain professions for women, were only present in some of the journals or advocated by some of the women journalists. It appeared to me that while the women were unanimous in their support of certain issues, there were others that seemed more likely to concern women who worked out of necessity or by choice. Women in this category may have wanted more in the feminist agenda because the ruling class considered waged work as beneath them. Conversely, those associated with ruling-class journals seemed to have a choice whether to go to work and looked upon work or certain professions as not necessarily progressive for women.

There were other differences between what I identify as ruling-class women's journals and those representing managerial- or professional-class women. These differences were most evident in relation to issues concerning women's direct participation in the political sphere, conflict resolution or peace, support for parliamentary or extraparliamentary organizations, accommodation with the British or the West, Egyptian culture, religion, and language. As the various viewpoints emerged—whether from the inception of a particular journal or later, because many of the women changed their views and organizational affiliations over the period under consideration— a picture began to coalesce as to what an Egyptian woman should be in a nationalist sense. That picture also exhibited where professional women consented to the elite women's construct and where they resisted it.

This nationalist construct involved economic, political, cultural, and epistemological concerns that seemed to break down along class lines in the journals. However, for the purposes of this work, class, as a term, is not reducible a priori to economics alone, but includes political and social aspects as well with the understanding that these aspects intersect with each other without any one receiving primacy. Furthermore, it must be acknowledged that throughout history, people from a certain socioeconomic class have represented the interests of other classes. Therefore, when I refer to class in this work, it is a relational term; that is, the person relates to and represents a particular class though economically may come from an entirely different class. Equally, women from different classes do not always conflict; at various periods in history, like the one under consideration here, women have achieved a certain level of cross-class alliance. As such, this work will explore the dialectic between women who represent two opposing classes and examine the issues on where there is agreement and disagreement. This analysis requires an understanding of what I term *upper* or *ruling class* and *managerial* or *professional class.*

The composition of the ruling class in Egypt during the interwar period is well documented. Ra'uf 'Abbas has shown that Egyptian agriculture formed the basis of capitalism in Egypt and that it was linked to all other forms of capital, including banks (both Egyptian and foreign), commerce, and industry (1986, 16–17).[26] A few large landowning families controlled close to 40 percent of the cultivatable land in Egypt in 1938 (16). Descendents of Muhammad 'Ali possessed the most land, with other prominent families owning several thousand *feddans* or more (Barakat 1978, 22–23). The influence of the large landowning families was not confined to the economic sector. After the 1923 constitution and the establishment of the liberal nationalist state, large landowners made up a significant proportion of the government from 1924 to 1950 that included membership in parliament, the ministries, and the developing parliamentary political parties (Barakat 1978, 64; Dasuqi 1981). The control that the large landowning families wielded in the economic and political spheres

26. Vitalis 1995 also explores the relationship between the landed aristocracy and other capitalist interests in Egypt during this period.

extended to the social sphere as well ('Abbas and Dasuqi 1998, 264). The power of the large landowning families, connected to the commercial and industrial elites, was so extensive as to qualify this group as a ruling class in Egypt during the interwar period. To secure their hegemony over other Egyptians and their hold on the liberal nationalist state, the ruling class needed to create and reify a state culture in order to gain consensus from other Egyptians to their rule.

In this respect, institutional feminism became part of the new state culture and advanced a construct of women amenable to the ruling class's interests. Professional women who sought to improve their fortunes allied, at times, with women from the large landowning families, including Huda Sha'rawi, and women from the commercial and industrial elites in support of the institutional feminist agenda. Conversely, ruling-class women sought cross-class alliances with lower-class women that aided their agendas when they entered public space in 1919.[27] By acknowledging the fluidity of the term *ruling class* and the reality that this class often allied itself with lower-class interests, this work does not employ stratification theory.[28]

Similarly, my use of the term *managerial* or *professional* class is also relational. The term *lower middle class* or *petit bourgeoisie* has been employed to describe the old artisanal class that included bazaar merchants, shopkeepers, the 'ulema, and artisanal professions (Cole 1981, 389).[29] The development of Western style professionals, physicians, lawyers, clerks, civil servants, teachers, university professors, social workers, journalists, and entertainers (singers, theater actors and actresses) in late-nineteenth-century Egypt created a new class that had more social status

27. See Navarro and Korrol 1999 (88) for a similar analysis of feminism in Latin America and the Caribbean during the liberal period.

28. For an example of stratification theory, see Baraka 1998, who reduces a priori the term *upper class* to, for instance, wealth, taste, and style. She does not acknowledge support from some lower-class (by wealth) Egyptians who thought they could be/were upper class, or the upper class's cross-class alliances that would have necessarily impacted them and perhaps challenged their taste/style.

29. For another discussion of the term *lower middle class,* albeit in India, see Ganguly-Scrase 2003 (544–56). India is an Italian Road state like Egypt.

(notability) than the old petit bourgeoisie but lacked the economic clout of the ruling class.[30] After the 1919 revolution, this class sought to become an effective middle class in Egypt.

With the crisis of liberalism and the emergence of the large land-owners as the ruling class allied to the British, professionals were left with social status but without a political and economic status to go with their notability. Egyptians in the professional or managerial class began to organize with respect to this contradiction. The key to understanding this class is its connection to Egyptians engaged in professions. Thus, for the purposes of this work, the term relates to any Egyptian woman who sought to identify herself in relation to her profession, regardless of her class position, by wealth. Munira Thabit, Labiba Ahmad, Fatima al-Yusuf, Nabawiya Musa, and Ruza Antun Haddad exemplified women who came from or achieved a certain level of wealth and status but who still sought to engage in professions and to promote other women in both professions and waged work.

Yet, despite their class affiliation, nonelite women understood the need to make cross-class alliances with women of the ruling class in order to promote their agendas. They recognized the power of the ruling class and understood that they could accomplish more with their help. This necessary collusion between the two classes did not prevent professional women from resisting ruling-class women on issues relating to their interests such as waged work for women or women's political participation. Neither the term *ruling class* nor *professional/managerial class* is rigid, reducible to a particular economic, political, cultural, or epistemological situation. The terms are fluid, as are the classes and the women in the classes. Each

30. See Hourani 1981 (88–89) for a discussion of the traditional notables who acted as intermediaries between the government, the ruling elite, and the populace during the Ottoman Empire. Khoury 1984 (507–40) expands on Hourani's work on notables in Syria under French colonization. Khoury includes the new professional class as notables who acted as intermediaries with the expansion of urban politics in the Middle East with the rise of nationalism. Baron 2005 (111) claims that elite women in the 1919 demonstrations were notables. As they were part of and supported the state, they could not mediate between the state and the masses. For the purpose of this work, only women who identified with the professional class are considered notables.

changes over time. It is not my intention here to explain why the women acted as they did but to show that many of those involved, on one side or another of the struggle, did not necessarily come from the side they supported, bringing into question the nature of class. Equally, I hope to show the complexities involved in their struggles that produced a dynamic interplay around the issue of institutional feminism during the interwar period, involving both an alliance between the classes on some issues of institutional feminism and conflict on other issues.

The necessity of this type of book is evidenced by the numerous writers who are frustrated by the dominant paradigm and seek alternative approaches to the study of Middle Eastern women and feminism.[31] During the cross-class alliance period from the early part of the twentieth century to 1970, feminist scholarship advocated the idea of unity of women, possibly reflecting liberal feminists' insistence that the answer to women's unified oppression lay in access to public space and the public sphere or cultural feminists' understanding that the nature of woman was the same. This approach became the basis for later feminisms, including socialist feminism where all women needed to do was to enter production (the public sphere and public space) to be valued the same as a man or have their homework valued the same as man's work (make private space part of the public sphere). Existentialist feminism and radical feminism reformulated similar concepts of gender as a category of analysis, one that was always situated vis-à-vis men and the masculine. The seeming unity of women became the theoretical framework, and most feminists merely plugged their research into this template without looking any deeper into the internal dynamic of the historical situation.

By doing so, feminism and feminists accepted the liberal project and worked within the liberal paradigm of men versus women by attempting to subvert it, women versus men. Feminists, therefore, continued to

31. For several examples of writers attempting to move beyond the dominant paradigm with respect to women in the Middle East and feminism, see Moghadam 1993, Karam 1998, and Botman 1999, though Botman challenges the dominant paradigm by resorting to a women's social contract approach or, in other words, the flip side of the same dominant paradigm.

construct women in the same reductionist manner that men had done. What had been missing in the feminism of the cross-class alliance period was an understanding of why women were allying with each other, since their alliance did not reflect a top-down feminism alone (collusion) but involved a degree of conflict (from below). The fact that so many feminisms emerged might suggest this but each seized on another aspect of women's condition without taking into account that different women relate differently to different issues based on their own peculiar social context. In short, women are as complex as men and are equally worthy of a complex history. This gets tricky with women of the Middle East, including those in Egypt, because they are caught in a double Eurocentric bind, oppressed by the inability to have history (modernity and postmodernity) and a feminism that merely recreates this paradigm for women.

Possibly the unity-of-women theory could hold as long as the cross-class alliance of women did and no retheorization was necessary, but by the 1970s and the introduction of neoliberalism, some middle-class women surged ahead of their female counterparts, taking feminist organizations such as the National Organization for Women (NOW) with them, and never looked back. With the breakdown of the nation-state in the neoliberal period, cross-class alliances that supported nationalism were no longer necessary. With the erosion of any middle strata—middle, lower-middle, and working class—because of globalization, little remained but an ever-widening global class conflict. Feminism, however, chose to ignore this conflict and focused on the power of globalization (global capital) to create a global unity of women. It also embraced woman as identity (postmodernism).

Postmodern feminism, while taking on the reductionist aspects of the concept of gender/sex/desire, still treats the discourse in an objective, essentialist manner while claiming to move it away from modern objectivity (essentialism) and confining it within a reified discursive structure, "a space of symbolic production based on the experiences, practices, and reflections of women, elaborated from the position of woman as a subject of representation" (Olea 1995, 198–99). The paradigm has not changed; instead of speaking about individual women entering the public sphere and/or public space, postmodern feminists have reduced individual, subjective women to a discursive practice; women are no longer only at the mercy of patriarchy but of those who have the ability to write or rewrite the discourse (theory) that the average woman cannot understand. Furthermore, the unity-of-women theory has changed only in one respect: its focus has merely shifted from woman to gender as a category of analysis, with gender changing mechanistically and remaining unessential.

Although the social structure has been given flexibility, the unity of the structure remains the same or changes only in relation to other cultural structures, not economics or politics. Thus, postmodern feminism remains in the cultural and epistemological realm of the Eurocentric feminisms that preceded it. It is merely the next step. Nelly Richard further elucidates this position with respect to women in the Third World:

> The postmodern discourse of the other is distinguished by its recuperation of the divergent and the alternative, of the minority. This new heterological disposition would appear to benefit the resurgence of all those cultural peripheries until now censured by European-Western dominance and its universalist foundation in a self-centered representation. Following the lesson of the same postmodernity that raised suspicions about scientific method we also need to *doubt* this new "centrality" of the margins that suddenly recompenses categories up until now out of circulation, such as the feminine or the Latin American. Feminism (the sexual key to the critical dismantling of the apparatus of hegemonic masculinity) and Latin Americanism (the dissident practice of the transcultural fragment) are categories relegitimized by the new movement toward the borders of the center culture. But women and the Third World are categories more *spoken for* by post-modernity, without obliging the cultural institution to loosen its discursive monopoly over the right to speak, without ceding to them the much greater right to become autonomous subject of enunciation, to assume a critical positionality itself capable of intervening (disorganizing) in the rules of discourse that determine property and pertinence. (Richard 1995, 221)

In short, postmodern feminism accords certain women— generally Eurocentric, wealthy, well-educated women—power over others through discourse. In the current neoliberal period, the cross-class alliance of women has broken down, revealing how a minority have become part of the modern/postmodern masculinist project while leaving the great majority on the margin. The emphasis on theory in postmodern feminism and seeming attempts to avoid essentialism has only created a greater chasm between theory and practice and between the women who control the theory and those who are victims of it. The result has been a crisis of feminism where these newly marginalized women refuse to call themselves feminists or even to discuss the "F" word.

This crisis provides a necessary opportunity for a retheorization of their struggles that abandons the concept of the unity of women, gender as a category of analysis paradigm. A new perspective would reveal not only collusion around the unity-of-women theory, but also contradictions within it. This may explain how middle-class, lower-middle-class, and working-class women, who played such an important role in the cross-class alliance period, were left behind by the 1970s.[32]

A framework of this type would require sources demonstrating evidence of where women colluded and disagreed with each other at various historical junctures, like the one under consideration here. Employing journals as the terrain of consensus and conflict, Egyptian women in the interwar period, who represented both classes, employed writing as a way to organize, communicate, and reify their issues,[33] agreeing on some, but

32. Some scholars who have retheorized the unity-of-women concept and examined internal dynamic in the liberal period as a way to explain the current crisis include Tax 1980, Frevert 1989, Spelman 1988, Marshall 1997, and Diamanti 2001. See also Ehrenreich 2001 for the effects of the destruction of the middle class on American women after the 1970s; Marcos 1999 for a discussion of the breakdown between middle-class Mexican feminists' alliance with indigenous women and both groups' attempts to remedy the problem; and Harlow 1992 for an examination of women's resistance as differentiated and the importance of women's writings in political resistance. Harlow's book includes Egyptians.

33. See Zeidan 1995 for a look at the place of the woman writer in modern Egypt. Majaj et al. 2002 views the works of Arab women novelists in relation to feminism, nationalism, postcolonialism, war, and transnationalism.

by no means all of them. The language they employed to transmit their discourse, however, remained decidedly an area of conflict.[34]

Ruling-class women employed French or Modern Standard Arabic, avoiding the use of the *'ammiya* in their journals, while those representing the managerial class often employed the *'ammiya*. Is *polyglossia* a gender as well as class issue? Khalid Kishtainy points out that the use of the *'ammiya* in plays and skits aided the development of theater and comedy in the Arab world. The rise of comedy and theater promoted democracy and freedom of discussion (1985, 80). These forms of entertainment also advanced women's equality by providing a means of employment for them by the twentieth century. Kishtainy further examines the links between this form of comedy/theater and the rise of the satirical press in Egypt that provided a natural leap for women such as Fatima al-Yusuf from the stage to the satirical press. This form of journalism often employed the *'ammiya* in its articles and political cartoons and influenced other popular newspapers and magazines.

By working as actresses, vaudevillians, and singers before World War I, lower-class women often acquired a questionable reputation in order to become more upwardly mobile. After the war, women from more varied backgrounds began to enter the professions. There were few standards, and the *'ammiya* was still prevalent as a medium of expression in written discourse, opening the professions to men and women of various classes.

Educated by Europeans in French, ruling-class women tended to employ French or, at best, Modern Standard Arabic, as the latter remained a more respectable language given its connection to Classical Arabic and Islam (Haeri 2003, 120). Language tended to relate to the circumstances of the women and to their needs. Where the vernacular became transformative for the lower class, who could employ it to increase their economic, political, and social position, elite women used languages that would provide

---

34. Sanders 1996 discusses the conflict between institutional feminist women writers and women writers who challenged the institutional feminists' agenda in Victorian Great Britain. Sanders refers to the latter women as antifeminists, a term I would not employ as it aids the reification of the already objectified and hegemonic nature of institutional feminism. A better term may be alternative feminists.

them with the legitimacy to continue to rule. These uses of European languages and, more specifically, French tied elite women more closely to the West than was the case with professional-class women (Reid 1990, 104).

The issue of *polyglossia* in Egyptian history persists to the present. Samah Selim, in her book *The Novel and the Rural Imaginary in Egypt, 1880–1985*, draws on Luis 'Awad to explain how the "third language," a vernacularized Modern Standard Arabic, became more dominant in narrative forms by the turn of the twentieth century, leaving the *'ammiya* to be employed in dialogue alone (2004, 39). Selim dates the end of the use of the *'ammiya* in texts when Mahmud Taymur stopped using it in narrative dialogue in 1927 (2004, 39). However, an analysis of its displacement in Egypt by the third language is problematic. In the first place, it does not take into account the writer's subjective relationship with the language. Not all writers employed the *'ammiya* because they thought it was the national (natural for Egyptians) language. Selim demonstrates that Ya'qub Sannu' wrote plays exclusively in the *'ammiya* for aesthetic purposes because he believed that it was the natural language of the theater, while 'Abdallah al-Nadim wrote skits in a combination of the *fusha* and the *'ammiya* simply to get his reformist message across to the Egyptian populace (2004, 36–37).

Interestingly, Mahmud Taymur had a similar relationship with the *'ammiya* as al-Nadim. He wrote to a friend, Julius (Abdul-Karim) Germanus, a Hungarian professor, explaining that he wrote in the *'ammiya* strictly for didactic purposes (Hejazi 2006, 4). Both al-Nadim and Taymur employed it as a tool to educate the Egyptian masses. Taymur renounced its use in narrative and dialogue when he entered the prestigious Arabic Language Academy. By then, Taymur had become part of the hegemonic group of Egyptian intellectuals who supported the use of Modern Standard Arabic and/or the third language as the hegemonic national language. Given that Taymur's relationship to the *'ammiya* was merely one of convenience, his renunciation of the vernacular was probably not much of an issue. Selim acknowledges that with the development of a hegemonic national discourse, the *'ammiya* became an "extra-national, subaltern textual language, occasionally and strategically employed by uneducated women, urban riff-raff, and, of course the peasant" (2004, 42). Selim admits, however, that other writers, such as Tawfiq al-Hakim, Yusuf Idris, and 'Abd al-Rahman al-Sharqawi, continued to employ the *'ammiya* in their writings (2004, 39).

The persistence of *polyglossia* in Egypt suggests that the issue was not resolved by the 1930s. The *'ammiya* was most prevalent in the theater and in the theater's progeny, the satirical press. The satirical press continued to employ it in *zajal* form, in political cartoons, and in articles. Most of the humor was directed against the political, economic, and social/intellectual establishment. Great intellectuals of the period, including Muhammad Husayn Haykal and Taha Husayn, were often targets of the satirical press, especially by the latter part of the 1920s and into the 1930s (Kishtainy 1985, 80, 88–89). While the third language may have been gaining prominence among Egypt's growing literati, the *'ammiya* remained an alternative discourse of dissent, especially in the satirical press of the period.

Something was happening here that begs an explanation. Perhaps part of the failure of liberalism involved the professional class. In the earlier period, Egyptians' access to the professions of entertainment, journalism, teaching, and nursing required little, if any, formal training. With the growing standardization of the professions that favored the elite and men, many who lacked training and who could not afford to be trained became marginalized from the professions.[35] Many of these outlets had been democratizing for lower-class women. When the standardization of them slowed this movement, it resulted in the breakdown of the cross-class alliance of women. Institutional feminism in Egypt could no longer represent all Egyptian women. As language, the means for the transmission of knowledge in the professions also became more standardized, the fight to keep the *'ammiya* alive became part of the opposition to the creation of economic, political, and social/epistemological forms of national hegemony in Egypt during this period.

---

35. See Landau 1958 (104–6) for a discussion of the growing standardization of the theater profession after the First World War. Landau states that while amateurs continued to audition for the theater, they were losing out to actors and actresses who were formally trained. Similar standards were being applied at the time to other professions, including journalism, teaching, and medicine.

2

Egyptian Ruling- and Managerial-Class Women, 1925–1939

Toward a Differentiated Approach

Since the late 1970s, scholars in women's studies have employed a variety of methods in attempts to deal with the subject of non-Western women in a more complex manner. Some scholars have focused on the sexual division of labor and the problems associated with "woman's work" in global capitalism.[1] These developmentalists changed their perspectives over the period from seeing Women in Development, a liberal approach taken from Ester Boserup's *Women's Role in Economic Development*, to a Dependency School–approach, Women and Development in the 1970s. A more holistic, socialist view known as Gender and Development emerged in the 1980s, along with the Ecofeminist Women, Environment, and Development perspective. In the 1990s, the Southern Women's Movement emerged and began to challenge the unity-of-women idea implicit in the former women developmentalists' perspectives, probably in response to the breakdown of the cross-class alliance of women arising from globalization and neoliberalism.

Part of the developmentalists' project was to begin to consider the nature of state with respect to women's development. Liberal feminists

---

1. See Visvanathan 1997 (17–32) for a discussion and outline of the changing perspectives of women, gender, and development over the past generation. Visvanathan begins with the liberal approach of Boserup (1970) and Leacock, Safa, et al. (1986).

such as Zillah Eisenstein proposed that the state constituted an area of struggle between patriarchy and capitalism without being part of it. Other feminists such as Michele Barrett also accepted the state as a benign tool of patriarchy and/or capitalism but focused on its instruments—laws—that promoted patriarchy. Meanwhile, structural feminists such as Catherine MacKinnon saw the state as the subject with no human agency involved.[2] Charlton, Everett, and Staudt, in their book *Women, the State, and Development* (1989), examined the role of state elites in the promotion of patriarchy. Although this work promoted more dynamic between people and the structure of state, it still focused on a top-down, male-generated patriarchy and did not show how women in the elite promoted an ideal of womanhood and how nonelite women both consented to the ideal and rejected it at the same time.

Another area of women's studies that sought to move beyond the dominant paradigm focused more on race, ethnicity, and gender.[3] The challenge to the unity-of-women concept and feminism was also an outgrowth of the breakdown of the cross-class alliance of women. Huge contradictions remained between white, heterosexual, middle class, and/or Western women who controlled feminism, and nonwhite, nonelite, lesbian, bisexual, transgendered, and/or non-Western women. This trend in women's studies challenged the reified discourse of feminism as a theoretical framework and provided an opportunity to deconstruct it in order to posit a multiplicity of feminisms and experiences that women themselves present/represent in its place.[4] However, this new experiment shifted the focus from locating women's oppression in economic and political arenas that were becoming essentially more global in nature to cultural arenas that were more local. Identity was now to be found at home in relation to

2. See Charlton, Everett, and Staudt 1989 (7–12) for an overview of how women scholars have experimented with the concept of women's relationship to the state.

3. See Davis 1983 for the origin of this genre of women's studies.

4. Drawing on Spivak 1987, women's studies began to consider Third World and other marginalized women's relationship to Western, Eurocentric discursive feminism and explored new ways to present (write)/represent (rewrite) these women through textual productions.

how women presented or represented themselves through cultural productions.[5] The discursive practice that Edward Said challenged in 1979 became the framework for postmodern women's studies, even in the Middle East. What has emerged from this paradigm is a multiplicity of women, genders, and feminisms that have no connection to each other, politics, economics, or anything else for that matter.

Furthermore, the new approach has produced great theoretical works in the realm of deconstruction but little in the way of reconstruction that would provide an example of what postmodern feminists believed happened instead of only what they believe did not happen. What is deterministic in this new women's experiment is culture. Gender has a genealogy; people do not.[6] Language, psychology, religion, and social traditions are the focus of postmodern feminism with each structure given a mechanism unto itself detached from any other considerations. Narratives of structures replace those of individuals. Ethnographies are possible in postmodern feminism; history is not.[7]

Although many of the experiments since the late 1970s in the field of women's studies have added to our understanding of how to provide a thorough and complex analysis of the role of women in various historical

5. An example of this perspective is Mohanty, Russo, and Torres 1991. While a multiplicity of women and feminisms became possible, gender and patriarchy became more reified around other cultural structures, language, race, ethnicity, and psychology, reflecting few analyses on internal dynamic between women in particular historical contexts.

6. Employing the ideas of the French postmodernists Michel Foucault, Jacques Derrida, and Jacques Lacan, postmodern feminists focus on gender as a discursive space and time mediated by culture, language, psychology, and cultural traditions. If men's gender and genealogy of gender robbed women of subjectivity, women had to reclaim their own subjectivity (identity) through their gender. Gender or social structure, however, seems deterministic here and the radical feminist genre of the modern period (men vs. women) has made a linear trajectory to the postmodern (gender vs. gender). Again, internal dynamic that would acknowledge conflict among women (gender) is missing. For an example of this perspective, see Irigaray 1993.

7. The effect of postmodernism in women's studies has been to ignore internal dynamic within historical contexts and to confine women to ethnographies, away from historical treatment—an epistemological marginality that is both masculinist and Eurocentric. For an example of this ethnographic treatment of women, see Stern 1995.

situations, many of these attempts have been successful only in identify-
ing one aspect of their condition, be it economic or political or cultural,
and they have done so by assuming a unified vision of the female gender,
usually as marginal or subaltern, without examining how women related
differently to economic, political, or cultural structures and how part of
this relationship was not and is not a unified one. Some scholars have
experimented with analyses of how various women struggled over similar
issues in a particular time period, but most of these works seem to involve
the history of European or American women.[8]

The history of Egyptian ruling-class feminism was not a static phenomenon that mechanistically transformed Egyptian society from the top
down. Instead, it involved change and conflict between women of the ruling and lower classes. After the 1919 revolution, a ruling elite emerged
with the old landed aristocracy engaged in agricultural production for
export, particularly in Lower Egypt. The ruling elite's maintenance of feudal relations in the Sa'id provided them with a steady stream of migrant
labor that enabled them to generate superprofits, which they invested in
commerce and industry with the Egyptian and Egyptianized Levantine/
European upper middle class. The circumscription of native Egyptian
capitalist development by the aristocracy, allied to the palace, and the
British colonial presence prevented the nationalist party, the Wafd, from
creating an effective liberal movement in Egypt even though disinherited
Egyptians counted on the Wafd to help them achieve greater social mobility. This breakdown began to occur when many landowners and intellectuals left the Wafd to join the Liberal Constitutionalist party founded by
Adli Yakan in 1922. The party, at times, allied with the Wafd and, at other
times, allied with the palace through the 1920s and 1930s.

As a result, the aristocracy maintained its hegemonic position in
Egyptian society allied to upper-middle-class elements: Egyptian, foreign,
and Levantine Egyptian. This new ruling elite created a parliamentary
monarchy—in effect, a new Egyptian state after 1922. This peculiar alliance of the large landowners with often nonindigenous commercial and

8. See notes 26 and 27 in chapter 1 for writers who have already moved in this direction. Also see Stansell 1994.

industrial capitalists effectively prohibited a type of middle class, extant in Great Britain or the United States, from forming in Egypt, hence my use of the term *upper middle class* for this aborted middle-class group. With the upper middle class in alliance with the large landowners and both in control of capital and the state, the professional class, though powerful as a result of its discursive notability and its role as mediators between the state and the general populace, was unable to secure a true economic middle-class status and began to resist the ruling class.

Elite women took part in the consolidation of their hegemonic position in Egyptian civil society with the men of their class by employing a Western form of cultural feminism. Through this means, these women created a construct of woman and a discourse of feminism that, while not incorporated into secular law, did become part of the new state culture. In the nineteenth century, elite women had already begun to exercise some control over the institutions of civil society, including schools, the media, philanthropic venues, and social work from their private space of the harem. Through these institutions, they could persuade lower-class women and men to consent to their image of Egyptian womanhood. Cultural feminism, as an institution, provided them with the ability to continue these activities in public space outside of the harem after 1919.

Although elite women enjoyed hegemony in civil society and were able to persuade lower-class Egyptians to consent to their ideal of womanhood and their discourse of feminism, they were unable to convince their male counterparts to incorporate them and their feminist agenda into the secular law of the new state. As a result, Wafdist, Liberal Constitutionalist, and monarchial governments supported secular laws for men while denying them to women; men had rights under secular law while women continued to have responsibility under Islamic law. In this way, ruling-class women found themselves in a dual position, occupying a hegemonic role in civil society that they sought to maintain with their male counterparts, but also occupying a similar position as lower-class women with respect to secular law.

As a result, women of the elite responded not only to their class position but also to their lesser position as women. As such, they employed their construct of woman and their discourse of feminism as a means of maintaining the new Egyptian state and the hegemonic position of their class in Egyptian civil society.[9] At the same time, they also employed these means as a form of resistance toward elite men who controlled the state by blocking their access to secular law. Elite women supported the liberal nationalism of the Wafd and, along with the lower-class Egyptians, became disappointed by the Wafd's unwillingness to incorporate their agenda into law. In this resistance, both elite and professional women were allied in their attempts to convince the men of the state to put women and their issues into secular law.[10]

There were other examples of cross-class alliances between these women in the 1920s. As elite women began to occupy public space, they became increasingly more concerned with transforming that space to their standards and, as a result, gained more direct control of the people in that space, including other women. They reached out to lower-class women in the form of various philanthropic activities and aided professional women's agendas and organizations. For managerial women's part, they consented to the institutional feminist agenda on issues that directly benefited women, including philanthropic work to aid the poor and widening educational opportunities. They also stood to gain from the discursive practice of institutional feminism when it sought to make elite men perform the same responsibilities as everyone else in Egyptian society.

Alternatively, given that elite women's construct of woman and their discourse of feminism served to maintain their class in a hegemonic position in Egypt, managerial women's consent to this national ideal of womanhood was tempered by resistance. Though Egyptian ruling-class men did not, on the whole, incorporate feminist agendas into law, they did not attempt to eradicate this feminism or its official organization, the Egyptian

9. Peter Gran suggests that gender contradiction in Italian Road states, such as Egypt, is not as important as it is in democracies (1996). If this is the case, then it may explain ruling-class women's ability to work with their male counterparts while still appealing to women of the lower classes.

10. See Hatem 1989b (186) for the alliance of upper-class and middle-class women in Egypt in their attempts to gain the support of men of the state to put the feminist agenda into law.

Feminist Union. They relied on both to garner consent from the lower classes to their hegemony and the state that they controlled. Elite women's attempts at bringing the newly bourgeoisified sphere of the harem into public space had a direct impact on lower-class women who already controlled that space and desired access to the public sphere. Their response was to counter housewifization by promoting alternative constructs of woman as waged workers and professionals.

With the failure of the liberal nationalist Wafd to expand Egyptian civil society economically and politically, and with the collapse of the cotton economy, the cross-class alliance of Egyptian women began to crack by 1930. As a result, elite women decided not to challenge the Egyptian state directly. They turned their attention away from the internal conflicts and concentrated instead on issues related to peace and conflict resolution, allying with Arab women and with other cultural feminists in the world.[11] Professional women, in contrast, remained committed to challenging the Egyptian state directly by supporting or joining extraparliamentary organizations.[12] These females sought to subvert directly the state and cultural feminism on which it relied, including the hegemonic construct of woman created and maintained by elite women. The nonelite also created alternative constructs of woman to challenge the national ideal and developed a discourse that aided the reification of their constructs.

Earlier works on Egyptian feminism had proceeded from the position that the construct of woman created by the institutional feminists was progressive for all Egyptian women and could be employed as a sustainable theoretical framework. The result was either collusion without resistance or simply divergence. Instead of viewing this feminism and its construct as part of an ongoing historical process, many scholars consented to the

11. See Badran 1995 (223–50) for a comprehensive study of the feminists' activities with respect to peace initiatives, alliances with Arab women, and their involvement in the international women's movement in the 1930s.

12. Baron 2005 (182–88) portrays Fatima al-Yusuf and Munira Thabit as women nationalists allied to the Wafd and Wafdist women, including Huda Sha'rawi, Esther Fahmi Wissa, and Safiya Zaghlul, presenting a paradigm of collusion among Egyptian women without conflict.

objectification of the concept that this feminism was as good as it got and could thus represent all Egyptian women. Judith Butler has challenged this method of understanding feminism as an all-encompassing category of analysis in her book *Gender Trouble*: "The feminist 'we' is always and only a phantasmatic construction, one that has its purposes, but which denies the internal complexity and interdeterminancy of the term and constitutes itself only through the exclusion of some part of the constituency that it simultaneously seeks to represent" (1990, 142). If, as Butler suggests, the cultural signification of gender and the body upon which it is written, as well as sexual desire, are constructed and thus at all times phantasmatic, then women and men are in a constant process of constructing gender/sex/desire and trying to make that construct a reality.

In this light, the institutional feminist movement and its construction of woman was not the last best hope for Egyptian women but only part of the historical process that involved all women and men and their constructions of gender/sex/desire. If this was the case in Egypt, then it is necessary to uncover the internal dynamic at work that necessitated a creation of an institutional feminism and construct of woman. It is also essential to explore whether women and men from less dominant groups only consented to the elite's construct of woman, aiding its reification. Or, with the nonelite's inability to achieve the associated political and economic advantages that went with the construct, did they resist it, too, subverting the hegemony of the construct and the group that created it? In a study of this type, gender/sex/desire as a category of analysis is intricately tied to historical processes that involve dominance over civil society and control of the state.

The Italian philosopher Antonio Gramsci has contributed to our understanding of the complex relationship between civil society and state. Like Butler's revelation of gender/sex/desire as a phantasmatic construction, Gramsci also exposed the concept of the state as political sphere, civil society as economic sphere, and underclass as cultural sphere to be a phantasmatic construction of liberalism and not an organic separation (1971, 270–72).[13] The dominant class in civil society creates the state, according to Gramsci, and, in turn, employs the state's coercive means—the law, police/

13. Salamini 1981 is a more accessible source for Antonio Gramsci's ideas.

military, and prison—to force people in civil society and the underclass to consent to the state (245–47).

Force is generally an ineffectual means of creating consensus because it breeds resistance. Gramsci acknowledged the role of state culture, transmitted through state intellectuals and civil society's institutions, including schools, hospitals, and the media, as a more effective way to persuade people in civil society and the underclass to consent to the reality of the phantasmatic cultural constructions of the dominant class (1971, 12). The reification of these cultural constructs through civil society's and the underclass's acceptance of them lessens the need for the state to force consensus since the lower classes are already regulating themselves. The control of the new state by the new ruling class is secure. Gender, sex, and desire make up only a small part of state culture but they are essential nonetheless.

In this way, the cultural constructions of the dominant class become reified, and this class achieves hegemony; the state provides the dominant class with legitimate means of force and persuasion. The state's control does not, however, only involve political and cultural activities but includes economic activities as well (Gramsci 1971, 160–61). This way the state is an economic, political, and cultural sphere as is civil society from which it is created. The creation and recreation of civil society and state involves, on one level, less dominant classes' consent to the ruling class's hegemony and, on the other level, their resistance to these hegemonic constructs through a creation of new constructs. Gramsci cited the importance of state intellectuals in the institutions of civil society in aiding the transmission and, thus, reification of state culture. The role of the professional class as notables in Egypt who at times mediated for the state and, at other times, mediated for other groups in the general populace, reflected this continual dynamic of consent and resistance.[14] Therefore,

14. Albert Hourani (1981, 88–89) discusses the role of the notables in nineteenth-century Ottoman Empire as mediators between the state and the people. Philip Khoury (1984, 507–40) explains how the professional class filled this role during the period of the French Mandate in Syria. As mediators, notables' allegiance alternated between the state and their constituents; hence they exhibited continual consent and resistance to the

both Gramsci and Butler reveal that the supposed reality of cultural constructs of the state and the dominant class, objectified through knowledge and the transmission of knowledge, are simply that—liberal epistemological constructs and not facts.

As exhibited, Gramsci denied that the separation of state and civil society was organic. He also denied the objectification of positivism in Marxism, highlighting the importance of culture in political and economic struggles. He did not accept the positivist position that culture mechanistically transforms from traditional to modern, but instead showed that culture was not superstructure to economic and political structure; culture could make or break economic and political structure. He called the interrelationship of structure and superstructure a historical bloc; neither were determinant in history (1971, 137). For the purpose of studying women, Gramsci's analysis is instructive since liberalism confines women and non-Western peoples to a nonpolitical, cultural sphere.

With a Gramscian analysis, however, the relationship of culture to economics and politics becomes much more complex. In this framework, even though elite Egyptian women consented to the organic duality of a cultural sphere for women, a political/economic sphere for men, and worked within this construct, a Gramscian perspective of their activities would reveal that they acted as much politically as they did culturally. Similarly, a Gramscian framework would accord Egyptian managerial-class women, who acted as mediators between the state and the general populace with respect to state culture, a political role because the state was not the only locus of politics. As such, aspects of culture, including the transmission of culture, language, or discourse, were relativistic and historical. Discursive practices in civil society, such as sexuality, gender, and

hegemonic class. Some of this consent may have broken down with the increased pressures of standardization within the professions in the early twentieth century and the development of a standard, national culture. With this development, some professionals were able to be part of the hegemonic class and the new state, while others became marginalized. With this standardization, the professional class lost its role as notables who mediated between the state and the lower classes. Those who were able to be trained according to the new state cultural standards became effective state intellectuals.

medicine, that could also be regulated by the state and discursive practices of the state, including law, were relative depending on who was in power and how such discourses would benefit their conquest of hegemony. Michel Foucault has explored the role of discourse or language in the process of reification of constructs by providing means of intelligibility and transmission, especially through socialization. Foucault explains, "All the more, one can, for a systematic comparison, confront, in one region or another, the rules for the formation of concepts: it can be done if one has tried to retrieve the identities and the differences that these groups of rules could have presented, in the Classical Period, in the Port-Royal Grammar, natural history, and political economy" (1969, 84). He locates the organization of modern concepts at a particular time, the eighteenth century, and place, Europe, and shows how these concepts became organized and reified through their transmission in language (socialization).

In this way, for Gramsci, Butler, and Foucault, the physical world and our cultural means of knowing it are not fixed. As a result, gender, sex, and desire are constructs tied to power and discourse. Women's position with relation to power and their role in socialization, the creation and transmission of language, provides the context for how they view themselves and others. This calls into question the concept of the subject that is also not fixed but which is contingent on power relations, as well as the subject's response to those relations of power. Thus, the subject/object is not a static dichotomy but a dynamic interrelationship. As discussed in the previous chapter with respect to class, women can and do change their relationships to gender, sex, and desire, sometimes consenting to hegemonic constructs of these reified discourses while, at the same time, resisting and subverting them.

In order to understand how elite women's culture and institutional feminism in Egypt with its construct of woman became hegemonic during the interwar period, it is necessary to explore the economic position of elite women between 1925 and 1939. Furthermore, it is important to establish how this class became dominant in civil society and was able to gain control of the Egyptian state. An examination of how this class employed the state's means of persuasion and the institutions of civil society to complete its hegemonic position, making the culture of the ruling class the state culture, must also be undertaken. Although this state did not incorporate the institutional feminist agenda into law, it did incorporate it into state culture. With this reification, elite women's construct of woman became and remains the hegemonic and culturally intelligible ideal of womanhood for all Egyptian females.

This process of hegemonic control by the ruling class was tied to material conditions, both political and economic, which began to change in the early twentieth century. In the late nineteenth century when Egypt was subject to Great Britain's veiled Protectorate, the British intensified cash cropping, especially cotton in Lower Egypt, which benefited the large landowners. Although the large landowners toyed with the concept of nationalism, it remained elusive so long as the British maintained the Protectorate because the aristocracy feared that the British would confiscate their lands and, as a result, supported them more often than not. After the 1919 revolution and subsequent end to the Protectorate in 1922, a new ruling class, dependent on the British military occupation in Egypt, emerged and created a new Egyptian state. The ruling class was made up of large landowners and an upper middle class comprised of European or Levantine Egyptians, who received advantages from the capitulations in the nineteenth century. They were allied to an Egyptian commercial elite—merchants, bankers, small industrialists—mostly from the rural areas (Hussein 1973, 17–22).[15]

The large landowners, in particular, whom the British supported, began to move toward agricultural production for export; some large landowners even began to invest in commerce and industry, mostly as speculators and financiers, but did not effectively become capitalists. As such, Egypt, during this period, experienced both a movement toward capitalism, especially in Lower Egypt, while maintaining a feudal character, predominantly in the Sa'id:

> The big landowners found it profitable to adapt themselves to the change brought about by extensive cultivation for export, but they had to prevent

15. For a similar and comprehensive treatment of the subject in Arabic, see Ramadan 1983.

a social or technological upheaval (this would endanger their privileges) so as to be able to perpetuate the precapitalist ideological and political superstructures which supported their privileges. (Hussein 1973, 20)[16]

As such, the large landowners continued to block any attempts by indigenous Egyptians from the lower classes to develop Egypt along Western capitalist lines. The Egyptian, European, or Levantine-Egyptian upper middle class developed within the parameters established by the aristocracy and supported by the British because any surplus money for investment came from the large landowners (Hussein 1973, 22).

While bound together economically, this new ruling elite had competing political interests. The large landowners were often allied with the palace while the Egyptian or Egyptianized elements of the ruling class supported a more nationalist and democratic outlook represented by the Wafd. The Wafd appealed to the disenfranchised population in Egyptian society, including the rural peasantry. Although the Turkish aristocracy did not support it, aristocratic women such as Huda Sha'rawi did. The Wafd, however, did not seek to radically transform the Egyptian political economy but instead opted for gradual reforms and concessions to British occupation. "The political framework (parliamentary monarchy) had enabled the ruling class to resolve its internal contradictions in terms of its overall interests and in keeping with the imperatives of British domination and changing political requirements—brutal repression (Palace) or demagogic channeling of the patriotic and democratic mass movement (Wafd)" (Hussein 1973, 67). As a result, the palace, the Liberal Constitutionalists, and the Wafd contributed to the maintenance of the political and economic status quo in Egypt during the interwar period.

16. Hussein states that the Egyptian large landowners opted to rely on migrant labor instead of employing a stable peasantry with small tenant farmers, and reinvesting their surplus in mechanizing agriculture and supplying technology to these farmers. These landowners lost the opportunity to transform the agricultural sector of the nation as a whole; they then had to encourage feudal practices in the Sa'id in order to ensure the continuation of this mass of uprooted, cheap workers for the export-oriented sector in Lower Egypt.

Although the ruling class primarily exploited the Egyptian peas-antry—largely tenant farmers or migrant/seasonal labor—or urban poor, it also marginalized the professionals. "The work of the minor employees and functionaries, especially in administration and teaching, was frag-mented and oppressive. Their income was high compared to that of the disinherited masses, but insignificant with respect to that of the big bour-geoisie" (Hussein 1973, 32). These professionals, during periods of crisis, allied themselves with the urban poor and peasantry in their attempts to challenge the hegemony of the ruling elite. They called for expanding capitalism outside its then re-feudal parameters, controlled by the Egyp-tian aristocracy, and they began to oppose foreign domination of Egypt by attacking Western culture (32). As a result, they ceased their support for the Wafd, became more anti-Western, and joined extraparliamentary movements in the 1930s (Khalifa 1966, 212).

How then did this situation affect Egyptian women? As discussed ear-lier, the liberal tradition acknowledged an organic separation of state as political sphere and civil society as economic and cultural sphere; Gram-sci attempted to deconstruct this dichotomy. According to this liberal paradigm, Egyptian ruling-class men alone had access to state, the pur-portedly political sphere. Their female counterparts were confined to the sphere of civil society and were allowed access to economics and culture. This arrangement may have appeared to the ruling class as a progressive concept, owing to its connection to Western liberalism. In historical per-spective, it would prove less progressive for women.

The old system of the harem created separate physical spaces for men and women while allowing for a blurring of the spheres. With the gradual Westernization of Egypt in the late eighteenth and nineteenth centuries, men's and women's spheres became more rigid and defined within the preexisting spatial separation of the harem. Aristocratic women's political power declined as a result of the development of the modern nation-state and its reliance on liberal positivism with respect to secular law.[17] Liberal

---

17. See Sonbol 1996 for a discussion of the effects of the modernization of law on women's reduced ability to access their rights through Ottoman *Shari'a* courts in the nineteenth century.

positivism acknowledged not only organic, separate spheres for state, civil society, and the underclass, but real, organic, separate spheres for men and women as well.

Nineteenth-century positivist intellectuals, including Qasim Amin, 'Abdallah al-Nadim, and Muhammad 'Abduh, promoted this Western idea of separate spheres for women and men in Egyptian public space. Qasim Amin and 'Abdallah al-Nadim were both students of Muhammad 'Abduh, a leading disciple of Jamal al-Din al-Afghani. Representing the *salafiya* or Islamic reform movement, they sought to challenge the aristocracy's secular and, increasingly, more Westernized rights and privileges by reminding this class of their moral obligations.

By adopting Western philosophical paradigms, including positivism and Social Darwinism, they promoted Western Protestant middle-class ideals of morality and thriftiness through more authentic Muslim and Arab means of transmission.[18] The liberal and secularist basis of this form of *salafism* made it more acceptable to ruling-class secularist Muslim and Christian women. One of the *salafists'* main targets was to eradicate seclusion for women and to educate girls to become better wives and mothers. Through social programs, women would become the driving force in maintaining authentic Muslim and Arab culture in the family and in society. As a result, they would be instrumental in the demise of Western cultural imperialism and, thus, contribute to the subversion of Western imperialism as a whole.

The positivist and Social Darwinist paradigm of the reformist Muslims, while liberating women from the private space of the harem, resulted in increasing the reification of the spheres between men and women, even in public space. The *salafists* actually believed that a separate sphere existed for women. Qasim Amin challenged aristocratic men by promoting the liberation of their women from the harem; promoting an end to veiling, polygamy, and divorce; and encouraging the education of their women

---

18. Cole 1981 (397) suggests that Qasim Amin was concerned with getting the Egyptian upper class, especially women, to become more frugal and better managers of their finances, similar to their European middle-class counterparts. If Egyptian women were able to learn these values, they could then transmit these values to their children.

in order to teach them how to run efficient households (Cole 1981, 397). 'Abdallah al-Nadim was an orator, journalist, and provocateur of the 'Ura-bist revolt in 1882. Like Amin, he sought to encourage aristocratic women to become educated so they could handle their finances and maintain their class position (al-Nadim 1881, 142). In an 1881 article, "The Training of Daughters in their Duties," in *al-Tankit wa al-Tabkit,* al-Nadim went on to suggest that women properly trained and educated would know how to act in public space and would be an asset to their husbands and society in general (1881, 142–43). The issues that *salafists* promoted were primarily targeted to women of the upper class (Cole 1981, 394). How-ever, the positivist and Social Darwinist *salafists* were more interested in promoting women's responsibilities as wives, mothers, and proper ladies than they were in promoting women's rights.

Al-Nadim continued this interest in the education of boys and girls in Egypt in his later journal series *al-Ustaz,* begun in 1892 (al-Nadim, 1994). He also provided the perfect model for aristocratic women to carry their domestic duties into public space when he created the first Muslim Benevolent Society School in 1879.[19] He later went on to create the Islamic Society of Alexandria, which provided relief in various social areas for the needy. 'Abduh, Amin, and al-Nadim were the primary role models for aristocratic women in their quest to enter public space. They showed them how they could continue their philanthropic activities outside of the harem. What the women found, however, when they entered public space, was that their "liberators" had been instrumental in confining them to an increasingly discursive private sphere.

The result for elite women was that although they had the opportunity to leave the private space of the harem after 1919, they found themselves bound by a separate law designed to maintain them in their new private sphere. Where Islamic law had acted as the legal means of circumscribing women's power whether positively with regard to economics or negatively with regard to polygamy and divorce, the new liberalism held out hope for harem women to expand their political agenda through secular law. After

19. See Herrera 2000 (7) for a discussion of 'Abduh's and al-Nadim's creation of Benevolent Society Schools in the late nineteenth century.

the 1919 revolution, aristocratic women were freed from the seclusion of the harem and the veil and were encouraged to enter public space, but they were not incorporated into the secular law of the new state. Instead, they remained bound by responsibility under Islamic law while their male counterparts enjoyed rights under secular law.

> In contrast to general state support for women's public roles and contributions, Egyptian governments did, however, resist pressure from women to introduce changes in the Muslim personal status laws regulating gender relations within the family. The nationalist ideology defended the maintenance of the Islamic mechanisms of private gender control as part of the defense of the national culture. (Hatem 1988, 412)

Though 'Abduh, al-Nadim, and Amin challenged the aristocracy's maintenance of the harem and aristocratic men's penchant for Western decadent culture, they did so by employing a Western, liberal paradigm that secured the separation of spheres between men and women in Egypt.

Elite women's relationship to their class position, then, was mitigated by their relationship to gender. Ruling-class women could accept the existing situation or turn to an alternative form of a Western paradigm to employ the *salafist* means to attain a stake in the public, political sphere. This would require them to perform their domestic duties in public space as a means of influencing that sphere. If they were to be bound by duty and morality, then their men would be bound by it as well. Egyptian ruling-class women could construct an image of woman and, as previously mentioned, employ the institutions of civil society, media, schools, and philanthropic associations, which they had controlled to a certain degree since the nineteenth century, as a means of reifying their construct of womanhood and convincing lower-class women and men of the reality of their construct. 'Abduh's and al-Nadim's work, in this regard, provided a foundation for their future activities. Gaining consensus from lower-class Egyptians would only reinforce the hegemonic position of this class of women all the more.

Elite men allowed their women to enter public space but discouraged them from entering the public sphere, even indirectly, while circumscribing their access to politics by maintaining them under Islamic law. In this way, they reconstructed the separate spheres, which were becoming more prevalent in the harem in the nineteenth century, in public space. Elite women, then, found that they had to perform duties to the new state but were not accorded rights (personal freedom) under secular law, while their men continued to enjoy rights and privileges without responsibilities.[20] Their consent to the reformist Islam of 'Abduh, al-Nadim, and Amin can be understood in this light as they provided means for these women to get their men to perform duties under Islamic law, thus according the women more rights.[21] As such, these women did not seek to move much beyond their sphere by entering politics or the economic sphere directly. Instead, they sought to influence the public, male, political sphere from the female sphere, a decidedly cultural feminist response. Their acceptance of cultural feminism as an antidote to their men's positivism, including the *salafism* of Muhammad 'Abduh, Qasim Amin, and 'Abdallah al-Nadim, merely acted to maintain the separate spheres in public space, though the women genuinely believed that their form of feminism was a mode of resistance to their men's positivism.

On the one hand, by working within the liberal paradigm and consenting to the reified duality of the state as a political sphere and civil society as an economic and cultural sphere, ruling-class women played the game as devised by the West and by their male counterparts. They believed in the reality that their liberation/conquest of hegemony lay in their getting access to the political sphere of the state, especially law. They did not wish, however, to enter that sphere directly, as liberalism and cultural feminism considered it a male preserve, but sought to incorporate

20. Peter Gran 1989 (14) discusses how the Muslim personal status law stressed duty instead of personal freedom, which became the preserve of men privileged to be subject to secular law.

21. Albert Memmi 1965 (76) states that the colonizer provides gifts to the colonized as a means of paternalism. It is not an obligation because once the colonizer concedes that he has a duty to the colonized, he concedes that they have rights as well. Following Memmi's logic, if Egyptian women were the only ones to perform duty, then their men could claim all rights. If Egyptian men were forced to perform duty, then they would have necessarily conceded that their women had rights as well.

their feminist agenda from their sphere into law, thereby feminizing the male, political sphere. In this way, elite women worked within the parameters of the Western liberal paradigm and of their cultural feminism and, in doing so, aided the hegemony of their class as a whole by contributing to the maintenance of the state's culture.

The ruling-class women's construct of woman became the national ideal of womanhood. To this end, they set to work on creating themselves as subject and reifying their subjectivity through a recreation of a Western form of cultural feminism that helped to define their construct of woman. Yet, by working to improve their status within the international Western paradigm, they came to accept the structure that eventually led them to recreate the increasingly separate spheres of the harem in public space. Working within the cultural feminist tradition, these women consented to the global hegemonic construct of womanhood reified by the West. As such, it further aided the goal of the maintenance of this class's hegemony.

Ruling-class Egyptian women secured their connection to Western cultural feminism early in the twentieth century and maintained it actively between 1925 and 1939. In December 1911, Dutch feminist Aletta Jacobs and American feminist Carrie Chapman Catt visited Egypt in order to provide encouragement to Egyptian feminists (Feinberg 1990, 70).[22] Aletta Jacobs had translated into Dutch Charlotte Perkins Gilman's *Women and Economics*; Gilman was a noted American cultural feminist (75). Two months after establishing the Egyptian Feminist Union in 1923, Huda Sha'rawi attended the International Congress of Women in Rome, which "remains an embodiment of the cultural feminist ideal: a model separatist women's network, unified by a belief in common female interests and values, and dedicated to extending that heritage into the public androcentric world" (Donovan 1985, 59).

Cultural feminism was grounded in European romanticism and American transcendentalism as a resistance to liberal positivism and

22. See Badran 1995 (69–72) for a discussion of the Catt and Jacob visit to Egypt to enlist Egyptian feminists in the International Woman's Suffrage Alliance, though she does not discuss the type of feminism that Catt and Jacob represent.

Social Darwinism. Instead of attempting to emulate men in the public sphere, cultural feminists in the West, who were more often than not from the middle class, sought to glorify their feminine culture and to employ it as a means of feminizing the public, male sphere:

> Instead of focusing on political change, feminists holding these ideas look for a broader cultural transformation. While continuing to recognize the importance of critical thinking and self-development, they also stress the role of the nonrational, the intuitive, and often the collective side of life. Instead of emphasizing the similarities between men and women, they often stress the differences, ultimately affirming that feminine qualities may be a source of personal strength and pride and a fount of public regeneration. These feminists imagined alternatives to institutions the liberal theorists left more or less intact—religion, marriage, and the home. By the turn of the century this vein of feminist theory moved beyond a view of a women's rights as ends in themselves and saw them finally as a means to affect larger social reform. Feminist social reform theory held that women should and must enter the public sphere and have the vote because their moral perspective was needed to clean up the corrupt (masculine) world of politics. (Donovan 1985, 31–32)

Therefore, elite women heeded the positivist and Social Darwinist *salafist* call to leave the harem and enter public space in order to become better wives to their husbands, who were already in public space, and better mothers to their children. Once the ruling-class family moved forward and was secure (i.e., with companionate marriages and women who could both manage a household and take part in the education of their children), then these women would raise the moral standard of the rest of society by performing their philanthropic activities in public space (Cole 1981, 398–99). Even elite Egyptian women and the Egyptian Feminist Union's call for women's right to vote was merely a way for them to extend their sphere through their feminist agenda into the male, political, secular legal sphere.

There was no real intent on the part of these women to physically work in this political sphere as they saw it to be a peculiarly masculine preserve.

Insistence on a narrowly defined woman's nature as wife and mother was their response to the rise of masculinist Social Darwinism that saw women as a separate and lesser form of human being. Social Darwinism appeared in the latter half of the nineteenth century and had a negative impact on female solidarity (Donovan 1985, 31–32). While ruling-class women consented to the positivist and Social Darwinist reformist Muslim agenda of 'Abduh, al-Nadim, and Amin in order to challenge their own men, they resisted the positivism of the Muslim reformists, at the same time, in order to achieve rights for themselves.[23]

However, elite women's acceptance of the dichotomy of separate spheres for men and women after 1919, implicit in cultural feminism, still helped them and elite men to maintain dominance over Egyptian society. Their decision, then, to continue to consent to this duality of spheres developed, not only as a consensus to the maintenance of their hegemonic position in Egypt but also as a means of resistance to their men's employment of Social Darwinism (liberal positivism) as a new discourse to control them. For cultural feminists, their construct of woman was rooted in the female's unique capabilities of reproduction and social reproduction. As such, the role as housewife and mother was emphasized and a cult of domesticity was created.[24] Women's entrance into education and philanthropic work was designed to make women better wives and mothers, as well as to allow women to perform as wives and mothers in public space.

The cultural signification of woman (gender), as defined by the cultural feminists, was a narrow definition based only on a portion of women's biological capabilities. Similarly, however, their concept of gender also corresponded to a reconceptualization of women's bodies (sex) because cultural feminists believed women's creative, nondestructive, and moral qualities to be innate (Donovan 1985, 61). By creating a construct of woman based on her role as wife and mother, cultural feminists also assumed that heterosexual desire for women was also innate. Cultural feminists objectified

23. See Hatem 1989b (193) for a discussion of how harem women took offense at Qasim Amin's criticism of them in his book *Tahrir al-Mara'*.

24. Badran 1995 (64) discusses the cult of domesticity as a conservative aspect of the feminist agenda.

their construct on the national level through their philanthropic activities and their support for protective legislation for women and children and, on the international level, through their support of pacifism (57–60).

Egyptian ruling-class women acknowledged that their sphere as wife and mother was separate from men's sphere, continuing the tradition of separate spheres that was becoming a feature of the harem in the nineteenth century. Elite women's entrance into public space after 1919 had little effect on eradicating these spheres. Instead, cultural feminists, in the West and in Egypt, sought to employ their culture as housewives and mothers to clean up and socialize the public, male sphere by attempting to end alcoholism, drug addiction, prostitution, illiteracy, and disease, especially diseases that resulted from an unclean environment. Their support for protective legislation, especially for women, can be viewed in this light. Their attempts at culturally feminizing the public sphere were not, however, to be construed as entering it but as a means of cleaning it up and, to that end, enabling women to become better wives and mothers in their own sphere.

Elite women believed in the universality of their construct and worked to objectify it through institutions in civil society including social agencies, schools, and the media. Journals, owned by ruling-class women, provided a means to create and transmit their construct of woman through articles and advertisements. The medium for their discourse included both French and Modern Standard Arabic, revealing their ties to the West and Western cultural liberalism.

Huda Sha'rawi, publisher of *L'Egyptienne,* was the daughter of Muhammad Sultan Pasha, one of the wealthiest landowners in the Sa'id. She married her cousin, another wealthy landowner and Egyptian public figure 'Ali Sha'rawi. She founded the Egyptian Feminist Union on March 16, 1923, and chaired the organization (Elsadda and Abu-Ghazi 2001, 101).[25] She was also a founding member of the Wafdist Women's Central Committee with Fikriya Husni, Esther Wissa, Gamila Atiya, Rogina Khayat, Wagida Thabit, and Ehsan Ahmed el-Koussi, secretary of the EFU (102).

---

25. Badran 1995 remains the best source for substantive information on the life and activities of Huda Sha'rawi, Ceza Nabarawi, and Nabawiya Musa.

She published *L'Egyptienne* in French, beginning an Arabic version of the journal, *al-Misriya*, in 1937. Ceza Nabarawi, though not of the ruling class, was editor-in-chief and a founding member of the EFU.

Angelique Ghorayeb (publisher of *Les droits de la femme*) and Labiba Hashim (publisher of *Fatat al-Sharq*) represented the Egyptianized Levantine upper middle class allied to the landed aristocracy. Hashim was born in Lebanon and migrated to Egypt with her family. She was part of the early Levantine influence in the development of Egyptian journalism but continued to write and publish after the First World War (Elsadda and Abu-Ghazi 2001, 71–72). Though Ghorayeb published *Les droits de la femme* in French, Hashim published *Fatat al-Sharq* in Arabic.

Tafida 'Allam, who published *Ummahat al-Mustaqbal*, acted as president of the Mothers of the Future and Egyptian Young Women associations, as well as the director of the secondary and primary schools of the Mothers of the Future Association (*Ummahat al-Mustaqbal,* 1932). She published her journal in Arabic. Balsam 'Abd al-Malik, an Egyptian Copt, also published her magazine *al-Mar'a al-Misriya* in Arabic.

Denied rights under secular law and still circumscribed by responsibilities under Islamic law, ruling-class women, by and large, were ardent supporters of the 1919 revolution and the parliamentary system hammered out in 1923. They sought, through the Wafd, the incorporation of their feminist agenda into law. The Wafd's refusal to incorporate their demands in secular politics pushed elite women away from focusing on liberal nationalism, as espoused by the Wafd. They increasingly turned their attention from Egypt toward a broader cultural liberalism. With the collapse of the cotton economy in the late 1920s, they became more involved in the affairs of other Arab countries, international cultural feminism, and pacifism. Though denied access to secular law, elite women continued to influence state culture. They shared a degree of political power with their men by persuading lower-class Egyptians to consent to their hegemonic position in the new Egyptian state.

As elite women were entering public space for the first time, they needed to reorganize and control it to their advantage, marginalizing lower-class women's access. They sought the assistance of professional women to aid them in their attempts to feminize secular law and create a standard, hegemonic state culture. In the 1920s, ruling-class women supported the Wafd with professional women, including Munira Thabit and Fatima al-Yusuf. Both Munira Thabit's journal *al-Amal* and Fatima al-Yusuf's journal *Ruz al-Yusuf* were pro-Wafdist. Nabawiya Musa was a founding member of the Egyptian Feminist Union with Huda Sha'rawi and was a delegate to the cultural feminist International Congress of Women in Rome in 1923. Early on, Labiba Ahmad also supported the elite women's cultural feminist agenda.[26] Professional women colluded with elite women to gain financial assistance and support for their own endeavors.

On another level, however, the institutional feminists' construct of woman and their discourse of feminism had a negative impact on professional women. Where the elite had been part of the domestic realm in the harem and continued to recreate, promote, and operate from it after 1919, managerial-class women had been joining the growing professions in Egypt, which effectively took them away from or changed their relationship to their domestic roles.[27] The cult of domesticity created and reified

26. Mariscotti 1994 shows that Labiba Ahmad initially consented to the ruling-class women's agenda but became increasingly more supportive of the professional class and the *salafism* of Rashid Rida and Hasan al-Banna. Ahmad is a prime example of a woman who came from one class but identified with another, challenging the economic reductionism of associating class with economic status. Ahmad's acceptance of Rida's and al-Banna's forms of *salafism* differed from ruling-class women, who followed the secular, reformist Islam of Muhammad 'Abduh. Where cultural feminists employed a Western paradigm and Westernized form of Islam to influence their men's control of secular law, Ahmad and the Islamists sought to replace secular law with the *Shari'a*. Ahmad and the Islamists collapsed the epistemological dichotomies implicit in the Western philosophical tradition. Economics, politics, and culture were not separate, and they occurred in one space, all at the same time. Women's space, even in the home, could be a locus of economic, political, and social activity. Mariscotti views Ahmad as a progressive force in dismantling the ruling class's control of the state. Though Baron 2005 goes further substantively than Mariscotti, she concludes that Labiba Ahmad was a member of the elite due to her economic status and that her Islamic activism limited women's political participation in Egypt.

27. See Cole 1981 (390–91), who cites Tomiche 1968 and Tucker 1979 on the negative impact of state capitalism in the early nineteenth century with the increased seclusion of harem women and the loss of their inheritance to male family members. While women

by the cultural feminists marginalized professional women by attempting to keep them out of the workforce, in one way or another, or by increasing their workload by adding additional domestic duties to their professional duties. Added emphasis was placed on this maintenance of managerial-class women in the home by their male counterparts, who insisted that their women not work outside of the home but become good wives and mothers like ruling-class women in order to lessen competition from their women in education and in the job market.[28] The professionals, who had not lived in the harem, were becoming squeezed between a liberal reconstruction of a women's sphere in public space from ruling-class women and a traditional appeal from their men, probably in opposition to institutional feminism, to stay in the home.

As a result of this bind, the professionals challenged elite women's construct of woman and discourse of cultural feminism by resisting the dichotomy of public spheres for men and private spheres for women in public space. Direct participation in waged work and politics were considered the preserve of men by cultural feminists. Women could influence the economic and political sphere of men from their position in the home, even in public space, and, at best, could work in waged positions that were extensions of their sphere. Women who worked outside of these

---

had new opportunities to gain economic status through tax-farming and inheritance in the late eighteenth and early nineteenth century, they began to lose some of their autonomous economic opportunities during the state capitalism of Muhammad 'Ali. With the rise of the new aristocracy tied to the upper middle class in the latter half of the nineteenth century, ruling-class women's position began to change. As their men became more Westernized and capitalist, it became necessary for harem women to be more educated to handle the managerial affairs of the modern, Western household (Marsot 1978). Ruling-class women's economic fortunes, then, became tied to the domestic realm and domesticity as defined by the West and capitalism. Domesticity became their profession both in and out of the home.

28. See Judith Gran 1977 on professional-class men's insistence on seclusion and veiling for their wives. While elite men were expecting their women to become more Westernized with respect to domestic activities, professional men sought to seclude and veil their wives, though their women had never been subject to seclusion and veiling in the past.

parameters risked having their reputations questioned and/or were considered aberrant. Munira Thabit and Fatima al-Yusuf considered themselves to be working, professional women. They were not only journalists but businesswomen as well. Thabit went on to become a lawyer. Nabawiya Musa worked as a teacher and in various administrative positions in education as well as in journalism.

Ruza Antun Haddad began by working in the field of journalism with her brother Farah Antun, publishing the journal *al-Sayidat* from 1921–24. She then partnered with her husband Nicola Haddad to publish *al-Sayidat wa al-Rijal* from 1925–30. Labiba Ahmad began publishing *al-Nahda al-Nisa'iya* in 1922. She provided the opportunity for many women to get experience working in journalism over the sixteen years that the magazine was published. As much as they may have attempted to consent to the hegemonic image of woman as wife and mother, they were actively engaged in the public spheres of economics (waged work) and the political spheres of the extraparliamentary organizations that appeared in the 1920s and 1930s with the failure of the Wafd.

Though Nabawiya Musa was a founding member of the Egyptian Feminist Union, Musa moved away from the EFU and became an outspoken opponent of the Wafd and a staunch supporter of the palace and the young King Faruq (al-Subki 1986, 69–70). The palace during the 1930s was also supported by the fascist organization Misr al-Fatah, whose Green Shirts engaged the Wafd's paramilitary Blue Shirts in street demonstrations during this period. Ruza Antun Haddad's husband Nicola Haddad had "introduced Marxist ideas in Arabic to the Egyptian public" (El-Said 1990, 11). Ruza and Nicola Haddad's journal *Al-Sayidat wa al-Rijal* reflected an antiliberal, Marxist perspective. Both Ruza and Nicola Haddad contributed ideas to the Egyptian leftist intellectual community in the late 1920s. Similarly, Labiba Ahmad leaned toward the Muslim Brotherhood founded by Hasan al-Banna in 1928 (Salim 1984, 122).

Professional-class women, like ruling-class women, also became disillusioned with the liberal nationalist movement represented by the Wafd. However, unlike their elite counterparts, professional women did not look outward to support a wider cultural liberalism, including alliances with other Arab nations and international cultural feminism with its emphasis on pacifism, but continued to foment their opposition toward the Egyptian state. Their opposition focused on issues internal to Egypt, such as the Anglo-Egyptian Treaty of 1936, and often reflected a militancy or support of militant activities that challenged the pacifism of ruling-class women. They attempted to disconnect Egypt from the Western historical tradition by emphasizing the contributions of Arab and Islamic women instead of focusing on the contributions of Western or Pharaonic women, as ruling-class women had done. Some also supported a less liberal positivist and more anti-Western form of *salafism,* promoted by Rashid Rida and Hasan al-Banna, as opposed to the liberal positivist *salafism* of Muhammad ʿAbduh, Amin, and al-Nadim.

Rashid Rida had gone beyond ʿAbduh in his insistence on building the Islamic community from the inside out. He tended toward a strict Wahhabist perspective of Islam that saw the West as an economic and political threat to the survival of Islam. The West was not a model to Rida as it had been to ʿAbduh (Hourani 1983, 230–31). Rida insisted that a government, based on *Shariʿa,* would make both men and women perform duty and, while women would still have fewer rights than men under *Shariʿa,* there would be but one law that bound both men and women (238–39). Hasan al-Banna went further than Rida in acknowledging the West's failures with respect to the rise of materialism and consumerism and the decline of moral and spiritual values (al-Banna 1968, 119). He admired and sought to employ what he considered to be the best of communism through Islamic means: an end to private property and class distinctions to achieve true equality (121). Al-Banna created the Muslim Brotherhood in 1928 to promote his Islamic agenda. Both Rida and al-Banna addressed issues that were pertinent to the professional class: economic and political marginalization. Rida and al-Banna attempted to collapse the Western epistemological dichotomies of separate spheres for men and women, religion and politics. Where spatial separation was a concern for men and women, their sphere of activities was blurred with respect to economics, politics, and culture. As professional women sought to maintain their position with respect to their class, some drifted toward the *salafism* of Rida and al-Banna and its antiliberal and anti-Western perspective.

Professional women's employment of Arabic alone and, in some cases, the *'ammiya* provided an alternative language for the transmission of their issues in contrast to the French and Modern Standard Arabic employed by ruling-class women in their journals. Their use of Arabic and the *'ammiya* may have reflected an opposition to an emerging standardized professional culture that was more Westernized and required more education, contributing to an even greater peripheralization of these women in public space and in the public sphere. Pushed by an emerging state culture that demanded that women understand their roles as wives and mothers, and pulled by the same emerging state culture that demanded that professional women be educated toward the culture of the state and its standards, many professionals who thought they had made it found themselves increasingly marginalized. Managerial women responded by not only challenging the culture of the elite but by attempting to hold on to real, essential access to public space and the public sphere through discursive means. The alternative was to collapse the spheres entirely.

Therefore, professional women's consent to the hegemonic construct of woman created by ruling-class women through cultural feminism was mixed with resistance to that construct. As cultural feminism made up one aspect of liberalism that had been incorporated into state culture, professional women's subversion of it through the creation of alternative constructs of woman and discourses was counterhegemonic. These women did not stop there, however; they also challenged the state directly through their participation in extraparliamentary activities and through their subversion of other aspects of state culture.

3

The Ruling Class's Hegemonic Construct of Woman

A Discourse of Cultural Feminism

Elite women's creation and promotion of their construct of woman helped them to achieve hegemony in civil society and control of the state.[1] They were able to accomplish this through their employment of philanthropic social institutions in civil society, including schools, clinics, *ouvroirs,* and the media. In this way, their construct of woman became incorporated into state culture, producing the national ideal that aided their hegemony and the state that this class controlled. The development of a discourse of feminism that became part of the state culture gave definition to the ruling class's concept of their construct of woman. It also provided legitimate means to persuade the lower classes.

Freed from seclusion and the veil, ruling-class women played an active role in this process. Through an appropriation and application of cultural

1. Much of the substantive information on the development of institutional feminism in Egypt during this period derives from the work of Margot Badran. I acknowledge the debt owed to Badran and do not seek in this book to challenge that information or to add significant new data to the subject. I do contend, however, that this study could benefit from a different framework of analysis that would move beyond the strictly narrative, top-down perspective scholars in this paradigm have provided to consider an analysis focused on the internal dynamic between women from different historical situations involving consent and conflict over women's issues. See Baraka 1998 for an example of the use of stratification theory in the treatment of the history of upper-class women who are portrayed as having no relationship with other classes of women in Egyptian society.

feminism, they reinvented a new system of segregation under liberal auspices. This system had a profound effect on lower-class women, including professionals who had not been subject to seclusion. As previously stated, elite women were less successful in getting their male counterparts to include their construct into secular law. Therefore, ruling-class women's consent to the liberal duality of spheres for men and women was tempered by resistance when the public, male sphere provided rights for ruling-class men under secular law but maintained a social, female sphere that demanded responsibility from their women under Islamic law. As a result, elite women challenged their men by allying, initially, in the 1920s with the Wafd and through their employment of the secular Islam of Muhammad 'Abduh.

The Wafd, however, was unable to become a truly effective democratic force during this period. Consequently, some women moved toward a broader cultural liberalism that included alliances with women in the rest of the Arab world and the international cultural feminist movement with its emphasis on pacifism and conflict resolution. This tied them to the Western feminist movement more directly. Therefore, ruling-class feminism became a discursive practice controlled by elite women, which they employed to elicit consent from nonelites to the hegemony of their class and to the Egyptian state.

The extension of a system of sexual segregation and a cult of domesticity that were features of the harem in the late nineteenth century ensured control of the lower classes in several ways. By replicating their roles as wife and mother outside of the home, they contributed to a construct of woman based on heterosexuality, reproduction, and social reproduction. Ruling-class women's reification of this construct promoted the domestication or housewifization of Egyptian women as a whole.[2] For lower-class women,

2. For a discussion of "woman's sphere" as an area of multiple and conflicting hierarchies, see Fessenden 2000 (451–78). See also Fernandes 1997 (525–47), who shows how the jute workers in Calcutta experience little geographical separation between public and private space, and that this gendered separation takes place in more sociospatial ways. Fernandes asserts that white, middle-class, feminist perspectives do not work for working-class men or women in India, as each sphere is blurred with respect to space and

particularly those who worked for a wage, this affected not only their role in the home and its relationship to production in general but also defined what jobs they were capable of performing outside of the home. Lower-class women's activities in terms of reproduction and social reproduction became separated from production, forcing them into an economic system of segregation to which they did not traditionally belong, a system different from the harem of ruling-class women who exercised control.

This application of segregated spheres to lower-class women followed them into production and provided more work for those who had to perform as model professionals on the job and model wives and mothers at home. The dominant construct of woman also dictated which jobs best suited them, limiting their ability to attain economic equality with men. Protective legislation, supported by elite women, limited their ability to work more and make up lost wages. Consequently, the process of domestication acted to maintain the ruling class's hegemonic position in Egyptian society. Furthermore, it provided for greater cultural and political control as lower-class consent to this construct implied that they were being good Egyptians in the nationalist sense. Also, as a result of the elite's insistence on heterosexuality and motherhood, they were able to create and objectify not only gender and sex but desire as well. Growing fertility rates that led to greater impoverishment was a predictable outcome.

Ruling-class women's attempts to extend the bourgeoisified harem to the lower classes reflected clearly the fluidity between state and civil

---

tied to other forms of spatial separation including that of class (bourgeois and working class). For an analysis of the role of the housewife in the international division of labor, see Bennholdt-Thomsen 1988. In this light, ruling-class Egyptian women, operating from a Western, middle-class feminist perspective, attempted to impose their feminism and construct of gendered spatial relations on the lower class. As this form of feminism and the resulting form of gendered spatial relations became part of the new state culture, ruling-class women were able to gain consensus to these constructs from the lower classes by appealing to their sense of Egyptian nationalism. In this way, the ruling class were not only successful in domesticating lower-class women and removing them from public space/sphere, but they were also successful in remaking the public space, thus controlling a space they once did not dare to enter without artificial means of spatial separation. Other analyses of this sort are available in Hancock 2001 and Predelli 2000.

society that Gramsci articulated. Through their construction and objectification of the "home" as separate from the economic and political, one which mirrored their belief in a separate, biologically innate female culture, elite women created means of persuasion by inducing self-regulation on the part of the lower classes that were as powerful, if not more so, than the means of coercion employed by the state through its imposition and execution of the law (Armstrong 1990, 67). In this way, women of this class participated in the hegemonic process. Foucault failed to consider the relationship between the creation of domestication and its influence on the development of modern social institutions (69).

Cultural feminism, then, aided the extension of the process of housewifization that was occurring in the harem to the lower classes. Cultural feminists created and reified a construct of a woman as housewife and mother through which they were able to ensure the hegemonic control of civil society and state by their class. An example of this construct was evident when the Egyptian Feminist Union organized separate subcommittees to attend to "the care and protection of children, health care, the promotion of morality, education, the reform of the personal status laws, to research the position of the Egyptian home, guide the mothers, the promotion of aid to the poor, to take, by the hand, women in Egyptian society" (Salim 1984, 55).[3]

In "Woman's Week," an article in the February 1935 issue of *L'Egyptienne*, editor-in-chief Ceza Nabarawi articulated clearly the ruling-class concept of woman and the purpose of the feminist movement: "The preoccupations of the feminists have far from detracted women from their responsibilities toward their family; instead, it has given them a better idea of the importance of these responsibilities—they can know and demand their rights without losing the charm of their sex and neglecting their home" (3). Features of the cultural feminist ideal included the

3. See also Rizk 2000 (14) for a discussion of the EFU's agenda to the International Women's Congress in Rome in 1923. The agenda included elevating women's intellectual and moral awareness, better education for women (including higher education), the promotion of more companionate marriages, the reform of secular laws along Islamic lines, increasing the age of marriage, and the promotion of virtue by cleaning up vice.

belief that women have innate characteristics such as charm, which make them more suitable for the home. This concept was keenly present again in the first stanza of a poem entitled "Woman" in the February 1930 issue of *L'Egyptienne*: "Woman! Frail and evasive is your happiness. She succumbs at the first sigh where love ascends" (4). The elite construct of the ideal Egyptian woman demanded that she, a cultural feminist, be sweet, charming, romantic, intuitive, nurturing, and aware that her sphere was the home.

Part of this discourse involved transmitting the elite model of woman as housewife and mother working without a wage. Irene Fenoglio-Abd El Aal, in her book *Defense et illustration de L'Egyptienne*, stated that the journal considered men to be the primary wage earners and that women would remain unwaged in the home (1988, 75). To that end, an article entitled "How The Young Woman Misses the Opportunity of Marriage," in the February 15, 1930, issue of *al-Mar'a al-Misriya*, counseled women on how to secure a husband, as that was their primary goal in life (4). Another article in the same issue of the journal, entitled "How to Achieve Happiness in the Home," provided tips for women to improve their skills as wives and mothers (6). In the November 18, 1928, issue of *Les droits de la femme*, an article discussed the issue of women in waged work and how it would affect qualities considered peculiarly female: "We know some masculine feminists who rejoice in these terms; 'We will have some rights and some responsibilities. The responsibility to work will be the first of all.' What will become of their beauty, their charm, this instinctive sense which gives them an incomparable power of divination? Will we again make ugly humanity in general?" (5). Ruling-class women believed that the cultural feminist concepts about the nature of woman and her defined sphere were progressive and civilizing. Lower-class Egyptian women were in need of the elite's assistance to elevate their own social standing.

Although the home may have been the primary space for elite women and the locus of their sphere of activities, this was not the case for lower-class women who had not lived in an increasingly housewifized harem, and who did not have a concept of themselves or their homes as a separate sphere. In addition, nonelite women did not necessarily consider themselves strictly wives and mothers or possessors of a feminine culture that transcended class, race, and both regional and ethnic boundaries. As a result, the elite had to convince lower-class women that their construct was somehow the model of the true Egyptian female. Their journals in this regard became an area where they refined this discourse and from where they launched their public involvement in institutions of socialization that provided them with the ability to effectively reach the masses.[4]

Elite women saw the application of domesticity to lower-class women as a progressive step that would allow them to gain a better sense of themselves. Education, therefore, whether academic or vocational, was geared primarily for a woman to get and keep a husband and, if unfortunately that failed, it would serve to keep women out of trouble. In a November 1930 article in *L'Egyptienne* entitled "The Young Girl and Work," this concept was apparent in the author's positive comments on the value of the *ouvroir* or workshop in Alexandria that trained women how to sew and then sold what was produced: "If these young girls marry they will become model companions who will be able to share their husband's interests and understand their real duties. It, therefore saves materially and morally millions of poor girls by teaching them a skill" (3–4). The journal's support for this school was understandable given that the Egyptian Feminist Union also managed an *ouvroir* in Cairo.[5] Mahmud Ramzi Nazim expressed a similar view in an article entitled "The Egyptian Woman and Mothers of the Future" in the March 13, 1931, issue of *Ummahat al-Mustaqbal*, stating that education for poor women should "teach them to know their womanly responsibilities so as to strongly prevent those women, who find themselves with obstacles placed before them, from plunging into the road of ignorance" (10).

4. Armstrong 1990 discusses the importance of women's writing in the creation of discourse and its role in the achievement of cultural and political hegemony.

5. See Fenoglio-Abd El Aal 1988 (68) on the EFU's involvement in teaching lower-class women hygiene and domestic economy. Fenoglio-Abd El Aal cites that from March 1924 volunteer physicians had established a clinic in the Sayida Zaynab area of Cairo, and the doctors reported annually to *L'Egyptienne*. For a discussion of how Labiba Hashim, owner of *Fatat al-Sharq*, aided Mlle Couvreur in teaching home economics and child-bearing at the nascent Egyptian University, later Cairo University, see Reid 1990 (55).

Given that lower-class women could not read elite journals, those in the ruling class had to employ certain forms of education in order to successfully domesticate them. Under the heading of philanthropic activities, elite women were able to actively socialize the lower class to become proper housewives and mothers, preferably in the home or in production. Their endowment of *ouvroirs* simply reflected a continuity of their former philanthropic activities that they had performed from their private space of the harem but which they could now perform directly in public space. Their efforts aided the creation of modern institutions in Egypt, developing self-regulation on the part of the lower classes.

Elite women believed that women were primarily to work in the home but understood that the lower class have had to work for a wage and should be trained in suitable careers. This cross-class alliance benefited the elite by enabling them to extend their woman's sphere into public space and the public sphere (waged work). In an article from the November 1937 issue of *L'Egyptienne*, 'Abd al-'Aziz Nazim Bey listed the professional careers he thought proper for women to enter. Suitable waged jobs included nursing, teaching (especially for the young), commercial work (secretarial), pharmacology, obstetrics, gynecology, and pediatrics (6)—work that was an extension of the domestic sphere. Through such statements, the elite discouraged lower-class women from performing work, especially waged work, that was not an extension of the home.

Ummahat al-Mustaqbal supported a similar position for women in the workforce, best expressed by the caption for the cover photo of its September 1, 1932, issue. The cover featured magazine owner Tafida 'Allam's picture with the caption: "President of two associations Mothers of the Future and Egyptian Young Women, owner of this magazine, director of the secondary and primary school for girls of the Mothers of the Future Association located at 41 Jazira Badran Street, Shubra, who works in silence without trying to draw attention to herself." It is clear that 'Allam and her magazine, which was supported by women of the royal household, promoted a construct of woman who, if she had to work, worked to extend the household and mothering to public space and did so as invisibly as possible.

An article entitled "Ladies in the Egyptian Police Force," in the February 15, 1930, issue of *Ummahat al-Mustaqbal,* made this point again:

The appeal to hire Egyptian women in the police force is a reckless appeal which is ahead of its time. I am not saying that this is the time to cling to the past but I am saying it because the Egyptian woman has not reached the level of the Western woman. The Egyptian woman still has before her various works to perform like her work in the field of education and social work.

Also, before her is the home and it is her little kingdom. (110)

The debate about Egyptian women in the police force was precipitated by the arrival on February 11, 1930, of a British woman police commander in Cairo, and the earlier arrival of six British policewomen in Alexandria (Rizk 2002a, 1). The women were employed primarily to police prostitution.

On February 12, 1930, *al-Ahram* featured a request by the famous Levantine writer May Ziyada[6] for a survey to be taken on the issue of whether Egyptian women should serve in the police force. What is interesting is that part of Ziyada's request for opinions included a leading question to the readers. Would the introduction of women into the Egyptian police force, she asked, contribute to "moral purification and the reform of public ethics?" (Rizk 2002a, 1). Ziyada's perspective was not all that different from that of the author in *Ummahat al-Mustaqbal*. For elite women, Egyptian women's entrance into the police force should occur not for economic, political, or social gain, but to enable women to effectively perform as housewives and mothers in public space.

This construct of woman was also evident in the fight for protective legislation for women that working-class men and ruling-class women championed in Egypt. Along with attaining a nine-hour work day and higher wages, workers also fought for special benefits for women, including not allowing them to work after ten o'clock at night (Salim 1984, 135–36). Protective legislation, though, had the effect of circumscribing what jobs women could perform and impacted their earnings. If women's

6. See Reid 1975 (97) for a discussion of May Ziyada's literary salon where she hosted Egyptian intellectual men, including Taha Husayn and ʿAbbas al-ʿAqqad. She also taught at Cairo University.

wages declined, they would have had to turn to other forms of waged labor, including prostitution and/or home industry to make up their lost income. The home, or private space, increasingly became the locus of both production and reproduction for lower-class women. However, unlike the previous symbiosis of women's production and reproduction in public space, this new relationship was not counted as part of the economy. The effect, then, was also a hardening of the division between the public and private spheres in Egypt.

Advertising Western style goods and articles produced in their *ouvroirs* in the magazines, elite women also aided the creation of the home as reproductive and social reproductive sphere (Fenoglio-Abd El Aal 1988, 107–8). Elite women's consumer fetish created desire for these items from lower-class women and men, turning nonelite women into quintessential shoppers. Social mobility became associated with looking Western, and lower-class men and women had to find ways to support the new consumerism. Yusuf Idris, in his short story "The Dregs of the City," exhibits Egyptian women's desire to look Western as a means to achieve social mobility with the character Shohrat, who becomes a prostitute and uses the proceeds of her profession to buy Western-style clothes and cosmetics (Idris 1978, 77–120).

Although ruling-class women's Westernized bourgeois construct of woman was difficult for lower-class women to model, its power for breaking down lower-class constructs of woman, both gender and sex, was undeniable and had the same effect as the elite's attempts to break down ethnicity in order to gain consensus to the culture of the state. Along with ethnocide, the Egyptian state had to engage in gendercide in an attempt to achieve a hegemonic construct of woman (gendergenesis). To achieve an effective nationalism, both ethnogenesis and gendergenesis had to occur.[7]

In gaining this power, elite women were possibly in a better position to create a construct of woman that would be progressive for all Egyptian

7. See Gailey and Patterson 1987 for a discussion of the negative effects of state formation on the autonomy of ethnicities. I am positing here that a state formation of gender negatively affects the autonomy and self-determination of women who do not have equal access to state in terms of gender, sex, and sexual desire.

women. Their cross-class alliance extended to helping members of the lower class become better wives and mothers, thus allowing elite women the opportunity to clean up and control a public space they had only recently entered. The institutional feminists aided this project by organizing and controlling a discursive practice that was becoming objectified on both a local and an international level. By extending sexual segregation, a feature of the harem and cultural feminism, into the public space/sphere, ruling-class Egyptian women also contributed to the international discourse of cultural feminism. As such, the value and necessity of bourgeois feminism was evident in that it drew attention to women's issues (Mies 1986, 208). As cultural feminism developed, not only in Egypt but internationally as well, it acknowledged a woman's sphere within the framework of sexual segregation as defined by liberalism. Cultural feminism, then, worked within a paradigm that ultimately maintained women separate and subordinate.

The contradiction implicit in Egyptian institutional feminism was exemplified in the feminists' decision to work with their male counterparts in the achievement of hegemony for their class while resisting personal freedom enjoyed by their men but not available to ruling-class women or to the rest of Egyptian society. Where men had recourse to secular law, women were still bound by the Muslim personal status law, which stressed duty instead of personal freedom that was the privilege of elite men. Elite women, including the feminists, attempted to influence the public, male sphere by reminding their men of their responsibilities and incorporating them into law. They did not, however, intend to enter the public sphere and challenge their men directly.

Employing the reformist Islam of Muhammad 'Abduh, elite women tried to persuade their men to perform the same duties and responsibilities borne by everyone else in the society. As a result, they challenged the personal status law especially with regard to a man's sole right to divorce, polygamy, and the minimum age of marriage (Salim 1984, 148–49). Concerned with morality, they attempted to regulate their men's access to recreational freedom, prostitution, and alcohol, making their men more accountable to them. 'Abduh's reformist Islam became the means through which elite women would accomplish this task.

'Abduh was concerned with the increasing imposition of European laws on Egypt. He feared that Egyptians who understood the European laws would oppose them, effectively leaving the country without law (Hourani 1983, 137). 'Abduh believed that the solution was for people to return to Islamic law and to become more moral. In fact, only men of the newly created ruling class were capable of benefiting from European laws that granted them freedom denied to the rest of the population. Although 'Abduh stressed a return to *Shari'a*, he wished to accomplish this within a Western, secular context. As a result, elite women turned to the secular Islam of Muhammad 'Abduh, which represented their competing interests as the ruling class and as women:

> Everywhere and at all times, Islam is the only just way of life possible; *L'Egyptienne* and its association the Egyptian Feminist Union openly claimed the reformist movement and, in particular, Muhammad 'Abduh as their own. Their theme is that problems, especially as they relate to women, all result from a poor interpretation of the Qur'an; if one was to refer to a good interpretation, that is, an interpretation by Muhammad 'Abduh, all the problems disappear. (Fenoglio-Abd El Aal 1988, 96)

A return to Islamic law, even under liberal auspices, acted to remind elite men of their responsibilities to their families and society. By resorting to romanticism in order to challenge their men's Social Darwinism, elite women could achieve two objectives at the same time. Projecting their personal sphere of the newly bourgeoisified harem into public space, the institutional cultural feminists could positively affect the male, political sphere, with respect to morality and duty. That, in turn, would yield the women rights, and they could increasingly remake and control the public space that had been the preserve of lower-class women. 'Abduh and his disciples, Qasim Amin and 'Abdallah al-Nadim, though all Social Darwinists, provided elite women with a road map to challenge their men's Social Darwinism and perceived (Western) licentiousness in order to achieve their conquest of hegemony with respect to public space in Egypt. Their men's maintenance of the Muslim personal status laws with regard to limiting women's personal freedom by stressing their duties affected all

Egyptian women. By attacking polygamy, a man's sole right to divorce, the House of Obedience, and the minimum age of marriage, elite women were redressing issues that had a negative impact on their lives more than they did on the lives of lower-class women.[8] In some cases, the women's reforms were more detrimental to the lower classes.[9]

Similarly, elite women's and institutional cultural feminists' obsession with vice through their attempts to prohibit alcohol and prostitution also reflected their concern with issues that were more problematic for them than they were for the lower classes. Elite men were in a much better position to afford these vices, and the resultant health concerns often impacted on their families. Ruling-class women, more closely tied to their men in the emerging Westernized, nuclear family, did not possess the same traditional networks to which lower-class women had access (Mies 1986, 206). As a result, they bore the brunt of their men's personal freedom more than did lower-class women who could turn to traditional outlets for support. Sa'ad Hasanayn expressed this situation clearly in an article entitled "Woman and the Prohibition of Alcohol," in the January 15, 1930, issue of *Ummahat al-Mustaqbal:* "The ladies should be the first to be praised for undertaking this significant project for they are the sweet victims of alcohol" (22).

Prostitution was another vice that elite women and feminists sought to abolish. The feminists, however, attacked prostitution as a negative aspect of colonization related to the dreaded capitulations. They also fought it on the basis that it was unhealthy and immoral. They struggled to end it through the broader cultural feminist movement and the International

8. Mariscotti 1994 (74) and Badran 1995 (124–41) discuss how these issues were more pertinent to ruling-class women than they were to nonelite women.

9. Sonbol 1996 (256) notes that the minimum-age requirement law for marriage that was passed in Egypt in 1931 and hailed as a success by feminists acted to also increase the age of majority to twenty-one years of age, increasing the time for legal authority over females. Sonbol relates that, in the case of wealthy female orphans, the guardian's control remained in effect during the woman's life and that these laws were part of a "state-sponsored patriarchal order." If this was the case, then Egyptian ruling-class feminists were as equally responsible for this order, if not more so, than their male counterparts.

Alliance of Women.[10] Elite women had a lot of support for their initiatives. Early on, Shaykh Mahmud Abul-Uyun carried on two campaigns, one in 1923 and another in 1926, though Abul-Uyun did not argue against prostitution by attacking the capitulations or by citing hygienic reasons for why the vice needed to be abolished, insisting that the practice was against the tenets of Islam (Rizk 2001, 4). Sheikh Abul-Uyun's second campaign in 1926 drew wider support than the first and led to the closure of prostitution houses in many municipalities (4). According to Rizk, the most serious detractors against Sheikh Abul-Uyun's campaign came from the elite women's own men in the Liberal Constitutionalist party, whose mouthpiece *al-Siyasa* insisted that "prostitution was a necessary evil" and that the solution was simply to strengthen the "moral fabric of the young in a manner that channels their material and moral energies towards noble endeavors" (4).

It is not so surprising that the ruling-class men of the Liberal Constitutionalist party did not support the end of legal prostitution in Egypt as they, along with Europeans, would be in the best position to afford such vices. What is more surprising is that they supported an approach to ending prostitution that was much more in keeping with the cultural feminist approach of their women. Elite women and feminists, then, seemed more interested in maintaining their class position with their men over the issue of prostitution and continued to attack it through cultural feminist means at home and internationally, and through nationalistic means by attacking the capitulations. Instead of debating the issue directly with their men in public space/sphere, they opted for more indirect approaches that would not put their own class position in jeopardy. They also did not wish to separate prostitution from hygiene and morality as that would undermine the

10. For an in-depth analysis of elite feminists' fight against prostitution by promoting morality and challenging the capitulations, see Badran 1995 (192–206). It is interesting that Rizk reports, of the few attacks against prostitution that the nationalists launched between 1882 and 1922, one came from an article entitled "The European Contagion in Oriental Countries" in the April 1893 issue of al-Nadim's journal *al-Ustaz* (Rizk 2001, 2). Ruling-class women seemed to be taking al-Nadim's lead with respect to linking prostitution with European colonialism and the capitulations.

broader cultural feminist domestication process that ruling-class women sought to extend to the lower class in public space.

In this manner, the creation of a construct of woman through cultural feminism was a necessary component in gaining consent from the lower classes to the hegemonic position of the new ruling class and explains the necessity on the part of elite women to create cross-class alliance. Elite women's active support for modern institutions such as compulsory education for girls, health care, and the prohibition of alcohol and prostitution had the effect of inducing self-regulation on the part of the lower classes, which resulted in greater control for the elite.

The elite's creation of a reified hegemonic construct of the Egyptian woman as housewife and mother became dependent on their support for compulsory education to promote good hygiene and morality.[11] As a result, elite women gained greater control of public space through their cleanup efforts and of the public sphere by limiting women's access to certain money-making activities.[12]

This connection was clearly presented in an article in the May 1930 issue of *L'Egyptienne*, entitled "The Feminist Congress of Beirut." Ehsan Ahmed el-Koussi, secretary and founder of the EFU, declared at the conference:

11. See Walkowitz 1980 (70–71) on the increased imposition of state control on the lives of lower-class people in Victorian England on medical and hygienic grounds with the passage of the Contagious Diseases Acts. Also Fessenden 2000 (459–60, 467–68) argues that American, white, middle-class women in the nineteenth century who targeted prostitution for reform often negatively affected the lives of working- and lower-class women in public space since the term *prostitute* was labile. Women fortune-tellers and jugglers were considered prostitutes; any woman walking alone was considered a prostitute. The effect of prostitution reform allowed for the entrance of elite women into public space. Hence, the domestication of lower-class women was part of the process of the achievement of hegemony for ruling-class Egyptian women. The actual claiming of public space, however, was necessary to complete their control.

12. Rieker 1998 shows how "urban renewal" in the Bab al-Amud area in Jerusalem became a site of conflict between itinerant street vendors, mostly female Palestinian peasants and petty-commodity vendors, and the Israeli municipal government. The effect of the reform project was the removal of these women from public space and the claiming of that space by the Israeli municipal government.

You have followed the example of Western women who have attained the highest positions due to their continual efforts and their firm convictions in the justness of their demands. Like you, they began by interesting themselves in some philanthropic work, to raise the moral level through their struggle against alcoholism, prostitution, and in promoting the physical health and moral education of the child. And while they have understood that they could not, by propaganda alone, influence public opinion and that it would be necessary for them to occupy posts which would permit them to have a voice in the legislation concerning these questions. Through their efforts they have taken this path and have succeeded in most countries to obtain that which they wished to obtain. The experience has proven that the collaboration with man in the general questions has never interfered with woman fulfilling her obligations in the home, but has led to a better understanding of her obligations and responsibilities as a wife and mother. (18–19)

The cultural feminist focus on health care in the home aided the development of hospitals and clinics in Egypt and revealed the connection between domestication and the development of modern institutions. The lessons taught in the *ouvroir* always stressed good hygiene. The editor-in-chief of *Les droits de la femme*, Alex Michel, wrote an article entitled "Féminisme," which was published in the November 18, 1928, issue. In it, he promoted suffrage for Egyptian women by employing the example of American women whom he argued had "beauty, health, liberty, cultural superiority, traditional authority, protection of the laws; the American woman has all of these things" (2). Michel also linked the development of health and hygiene to women's ability to access equal education.

In order for ruling-class women to complete the process of making their construct of woman the hegemonic construct of the state, however, they had to link their issues to the future of the nation. On the inside cover of the February 1930 issue of *L'Egyptienne*, an advertisement for the EFU's *ouvroir* reminded women that their purchases from the *ouvroir* were both an act of charity and national encouragement. In an article entitled "Women and the Prohibition of Alcohol," in the January 15, 1930, issue of *Ummahat al-Mustaqbal*, Hasanayn tied the women's morality campaign to nationalist interests when he stated that "the prohibition of alcohol is morally right for all Egyptians as it restores progress and prosperity to themselves and the building of their homeland" (22). Mahmud Ramzi Nazim echoed similar nationalist sentiments in an article in the March 13, 1931, issue of *Ummahat al-Mustaqbal,* stating that a solid, strong state would emerge in Egypt by educating the mothers of the future (11).

As part of the nationalist program, institutional feminism played a role in breaking down traditional constructs of woman and positing the elite's construct as the national norm. Elite women, with their feminist counterparts, attempted to clean up and make healthy public space in Egypt. Their war on alcohol and prostitution induced self-regulation on the part of the lower classes (Salim 1984, 59). This passive form of coercion would become more controlling with the introduction of modern discourses such as psychiatry and gynecology. In this way, institutional feminism became an important discourse for generating consensus from the lower classes to the hegemony of the new Egyptian elite and to its state. It aided elite women in gaining better control of lower-class women's activities in public space while also negatively affecting their own men's ability to take advantages of vices there.

Another way that elite women reified their construct of woman, according to the cultural feminist paradigm, was by their avoidance of any direct confrontation with their men and the British, opting, instead, to challenge both through an alliance with other cultural feminists in the Arab world and in the West.[13] This alliance promoted pacifism and redirected elite women's activities away from the increasing political turmoil in Egypt in the 1930s. Elite women's reliance on 'Abduh's reformist Islam as a model for their activities was problematic as 'Abduh was tolerant of the British and did not support the petty bourgeois revolutionaries Ahmad 'Urabi and Mustafa Kamil, arguing that Egypt was not ready for independence (Hourani 1983, 158–60). Ruling-class women supported the slow,

---

13. Hatem 1989a explores Egyptian upper- and middle-class women's employment of conflict resolution and also discusses their ties to the pacifist movement among Arab upper-class feminists and the international feminist movement dominated by Western women. Also see Mariscotti 1994 (79–80) and Badran 1995 (223–38) for similar discussions on the growing connection of Egyptian feminism with Arab and international feminism.

evolutionary approach to changing the political situation or changing women's roles in Egypt that their Social Darwinist men advocated and did not seek to confront their men or the colonial regime head on by directly entering the public, political sphere.

Most of the elite women's journals did not discuss politics, as they viewed it as a strictly men's sphere. The EFU's journals *L'Egyptienne* and *al-Misriya,* however, did discuss current political issues. Cultural feminists, including Huda Sha'rawi, could be found peacefully demonstrating or advocating boycotts of British goods in public space. Though the cultural feminists did protest in public space, they did not seek direct involvement in political organizations. They did not support the extraparliamentary movements that developed in the 1930s or the violent demonstrations that broke out during that time. They chose, instead, to respond to the political upheavals with pacifism that they believed was also an innately female characteristic.

As the political and economic situation in Egypt worsened during the Great Depression, elite women and the institutional feminists became more attuned to the pacifist movement associated with Western cultural feminism. In its January 1932 issue, *L'Egyptienne* ran a photo assignment entitled "The Nobel Prize for Peace" on Jane Addams, a noted cultural feminist (32). In December 1931, the magazine featured Mahatma Gandhi in an insert with the caption "The Apostle of Non-Violence." Ceza Nabarawi had accompanied the Wafd delegation to Port Said to see Gandhi off after his trip to Egypt in 1931; Gandhi had stressed the importance of women in the pacifist struggle for independence from Great Britain (Rizk 2002, 5).

In an article in the October 1930 issue of *L'Egyptienne,* Ceza Nabarawi appealed to the Egyptian people, especially the students, to stop demanding political rights from Great Britain and to support new economic measures instead. "Today, where the world economic crisis is impacting hard on the Egyptian market and has resulted in a formidable decline for our cotton," she stated, "only the same initiatives have been called for to save Egypt from the misery which menaces it. Along with agriculture that up until now has been our only source of wealth, industry and commerce must be staunchly encouraged" (2).

Similarly, Huda Sha'rawi exhibited a pacifist response to Sir Samuel Hoare's reneging on Egypt's right to self rule due to Italy's incursion into Ethiopia. The talks resulted in the rioting of students from Cairo University, where Egyptian and British police killed four students. In an article entitled "The Bloody Consequences of an Awkward Discourse," in the November 1935 issue of *L'Egyptienne,* Huda Sha'rawi stated that she was appalled as an Egyptian and as a pacifist and scolded the Tawfiq Nasim regime and Great Britain, demanding that they mend their ways (2–6). Sha'rawi acted as a mother, reminding the Egyptian state and Great Britain to mind their manners and resolve their conflicts. Like Nabarawi, Sha'rawi did not support the student demonstrations that were becoming much more violent.

Elite women advocated a slow, step-by-step process to achieve independence for Egypt. In their attempts to feminize the country, their political activities were generally pacifist and bent on conflict resolution, if they existed at all. Instead of allying themselves to a particular party, whether parliamentary or extraparliamentary, the ruling-class women and feminists attempted to remain outside of the confrontations. Their role as women, defined by their construct, limited them to their culture, a culture they employed to try to end conflict and not to instigate it. Active, direct involvement in politics for all of the elite women was, like waged labor, considered the domain of men.

This was the case for Huda Sha'rawi, in particular, who was not interested in jumping into disputes among the parties but instead called for unity for the sake of the country (Khalifa 1966, 23). Did ruling-class women's insistence on peaceful means, as opposed to conflict or revolution, aid the maintenance of the existing British colonial presence in Egypt for a much longer period of time? Elite women's unwillingness to come to terms with colonialism until much later was clearly exhibited in an article dated January 1931 in *L'Egyptienne* about French women who married North African men. In her book, Irene Fenoglio-Abd El Aal explained: "It [*L'Egyptienne*] not only does not take into consideration that Algeria is an Arab country, but fails to question colonialism and, in particular, the French colonization of Algeria which is not perceived as an Arab country but a country of French and indigenous people." In fact, she states that until 1935 there was little mention of Arab nationalism in *L'Egyptienne* (1988, 85).

From 1926 to 1929, she cited nine articles or instances where the magazine praised the Zionist movement without any mention of the Palestinians or Arab nationalism (86). By working within the liberal positivist episte- mological framework of separate spheres, elite women were able to chal- lenge their men and British colonialism from their innate, female sphere. They also aided the reification of the men's and women's spheres, mak- ing it much more difficult for Egyptian women who wanted to participate directly in politics in the public sphere. Egyptian women who challenged the growing hegemonic cultural feminist construct in this regard risked being viewed as aberrant.

During the political upheavals in Egypt during the 1930s and the outbreak of the Arab rebellion in Palestine in 1936, ruling-class women diverted their attention away from the internal political conflicts in Egypt and moved toward a broader alliance with women in the Arab world as well as with the international cultural feminist movement.[14] An article entitled "The Palestinian Problem," in the July 15, 1937, issue of *al-Misriya* (the Arabic language equivalent of *L'Egyptienne*), called for a settlement of the Arab rebellion to restore peace to the Holy Land:

> The problem of Palestine is the greatest problem that concerns all Mid-
> dle Eastern people. Palestine is an important religious center that brings
> together various religious denominations. As such, it was important as
> a place of peace and reverence of its shared holy, religious cites. We join
> our voice with ardor and pain to the voice of our Palestinian sisters in
> the protest against the behavior of the British government. (2)

Ruling-class women did not protest the Zionist colonization of Pal- estine nor did they understand Britain's role in the Arab rebellion that resulted in the undermining of Palestinian rights.[15] An acknowledgment

14. See Badran 1995 for discussions on the Egyptian feminists's frustrations with their Western colleagues who could not or would not understand issues that did not relate to them, including the capitulations and the problems of Palestinian women during the Arab rebellion.

15. Hatem 1989a (61–62) presents evidence of the alliance of upper-class Egyptian women with upper-class Palestinian women regarding the problems in Palestine during this period. Hatem notes that elite Egyptian women did not dismiss the British as allies.

of this type may have implicated their class in land questions in Egypt. As they did with the students at Cairo University in 1935, they sought only to scold Great Britain and to remind the British of their duty to the Palestinian people. Ironically, by extending their innate pacifism and role as housewife and mother to the wider Arab world, elite women diverted their attention away from the conflicts present in their own country during this period, allowing for the continuance of the colonial status quo in Egypt.

As they relied on Western epistemological foundations to promote their agendas, it should not be surprising that elite women chose Western women as their role models and sought an alliance with them in international women's movements. In a lecture given at the American University in Cairo entitled "The Role of Women in the World Development Movement" (reprinted in *Fatat al-Sharq*), Huda Sha'rawi traced the feminist movement from its inception in France with women such as Madame Dustal and Charlotte Cordier in the eighteenth century to the growth of the movement in the United States. She discussed the feminists' split with abolitionism and the work of the "mujahida" Susan B. Anthony (Sha'rawi 1929, 125–33). In the same speech, she encouraged the women to support the League of Nations in Geneva (132). Her affiliation with the International Alliance of Women for Suffrage and Equal Citizenship (IAW) began in 1923; she became the organization's vice president in 1935. "The Rights of the Woman," an article in the January 15, 1930, issue of *Ummahat al-Mustaqbal,* also traced the beginnings of the fight for women's rights from Mary Wollstonecraft's *A Vindication of the Rights of Women* to Russian writer Esther Gorsky (13). The magazine *al-Mar'a al-Misriya* discussed the position of mothers in France in an article dated March 15, 1930 (47).

While the subject matter of the journals emphasized elite women's ties to the West and cultural feminism, the language of the journals also reflected this connection. French was the medium for both *L'Egyptienne* and *Les droits de la femme.* Though *L'Egyptienne* was first published in 1925, Huda Sha'rawi did not begin an Arabic-language version of the magazine, *al-Misriya,* until 1937; the French magazine began an Arabic translation in 1930. Irene Fenoglio-Abd El Aal has noted that the presence of the French language in forty-four of the journals published in Cairo in the early twentieth century was not a reflection of a large French population in the city but the result of the Egyptian elite's decision to adopt the language for their own use (1988, 44). The elite's employment of French was deliberate and aided the maintenance of their class as hegemonic.

The other magazines, *Ummahat al-Mustaqbal, Fatat al-Sharq,* and *al-Mar'a al-Misriya,* were published in Modern Standard Arabic. Modern Standard Arabic was an outgrowth of 'Abduh's secular Islamic movement that included the reform of Classical Arabic to be employed as the new discourse of journalism. 'Abduh himself became famous through his columns in the newspaper *al-Ahram* (Rugh 1979, 19), as al-Nadim had done similarly through his journals *al-Tankit wa al-Tabkit* and *al-Ustaz.* The reform of Classical Arabic, while allowing for the maintenance of the language of the Qur'an with its neo-*Shari'a* implications, also effectively ended the monopoly that the *'ulama* had on Arabic. This movement peripheralized the power of the shaykhs, especially in the Sa'id, and ended any attempts at incorporating the *'ammiya,* the Egyptian vernacular, into the written language. The reform of the Arabic language, then, impacted negatively the nationalist movement and the lower classes that supported it. It also aided the reification of separate spheres for culture (religion) and political economy that the West sought to extend to the Middle East.

The form of the written language affected the construction of civil society in Egypt during the interwar period. Who was included in civil society was not only created economically, politically, and culturally but intellectually, through discourse, as well. The choice of a Modern Standard Arabic that was "practically intertranslatable with Modern French journalese" helped to reify constructs created by the new hegemonic class (Hodgson 1974, 3:291). Ruling-class women's journals written in French or the Modern Standard Arabic worked toward this endeavor. As such, evidence of the *'ammiya* was lacking in these journals, reflecting their high literary style in comparison with journals of the managerial class, including *Ruz al-Yusuf* or *al-Fatah,* which courted more mass appeal.[16]

The standardization of Arabic and its application in journalism helped not only in the creation and maintenance of Egyptian civil society but also

16. See Baron 2005 (205), where she states that Labiba Ahmad's journal *al-Nahda al-Nisa'iya* appealed to the "middle strata and professional class."

to epistemologically maintain the colonial connection. By acknowledging the organic separation of the written and oral tradition, and through the valuation of the written tradition over the oral, ruling-class women again accepted and worked within the liberal intellectual framework of Orientalism.[17] Adopting the Orientalist position, elite women exhibited a desire to be perceived as Western. The women's decision to employ the colonial language or the Modern Standard Arabic as their literary medium reflected their intent to create not only a construct of woman by which all other women in Egypt would be measured but a construct of journalism as well by which all other journals in Egypt would be measured. Ironically, they attempted to achieve this construct by distancing themselves from the profession of journalism that was developing at this time and providing instead what they perceived as a written extension of the salon tradition that took place in the harem. When aristocratic women moved the harem to public space, they brought the salon along with it in the form of their journals. Journalism was and is considered a low prestige job in the Middle East (Rugh 1979, 13). A woman of this class would not want to be associated with such a profession, let alone be associated with waged work.

In this way, ruling-class women and feminists did not involve themselves directly in the public sphere. They did not work for a wage, nor did they consider themselves professionals. These women expanded their roles as housewives and mothers outside of the home through their support of education, by opening and supporting *ouvroirs,* and through their philanthropic activities, an outgrowth of their contributions to *waqf.* Their housecleaning, too, was an activity that was extended to all of Egyptian public space that was to be sanitized, freed of trash, disease, and moral vices, including alcohol and prostitution. As cultural feminists, they wanted to modify and control this space. Their personal female sphere of housewifery and motherhood that they believed to be innate would serve to create a greater good there.

However, ruling-class women's actions in this regard were also targeted against their men, who could claim freedom under secular law. This

17. See Said 1979 (26) for a discussion on the role of the media in the reification of the discourse of Orientalism.

law was denied to women and the rest of the Egyptian population. If elite men could be brought to understand their responsibilities, they would surely grant their women rights. Muhammad 'Abduh, with his followers Qasim Amin and 'Abdallah al-Nadim, though all Social Darwinists, provided the framework for ruling-class women to challenge their men's license while promoting their own agenda. Consequently, elite women did not attempt to challenge their men or to access the public/political sphere directly via parliamentary or extraparliamentary organizations. In fact, they increasingly turned their political attention away from Egypt toward an alliance with Arab and Western women's organizations in the late 1920s and 1930s. They also continued the old salon tradition only in the guise of the new journalism, where they cemented their relationship with the West through their use of the French language and Modern Standard Arabic.

Though ruling-class women resisted their men's freedom, they did so through an acknowledgment of the men's Social Darwinist position that the women's sphere was separate and subordinate. Cultural feminism accepted woman's nature (sex), as her culture (gender), thus accepting the circumscribed sphere of the home or harem as women's innate place. As such, women could only function from that reified domain, whether it was actually in the home (private space) or in society (public space). This meant that only men had access to economics and politics (public sphere), and that women could only affect this sphere from their private sphere.

Elite women assumed that all Egyptian women would want to share their historical circumstances and the construct of woman they created. They believed that their attempts to feminize society would bring progress to Egyptian women as a whole. Those from other classes and ethnic and racial backgrounds, however, had varying concepts of what it meant to be a woman. Therefore, positing one construct of woman as the norm, the cultural feminist model, and incorporating that construct as part of the state culture, the national-centered model of woman, had the effect of breaking down lower-class women's constructs of what it meant to be a woman. The lower classes would then acknowledge the legitimacy of the state. Could this explain why ruling-class men did not harass or disband the EFU? Was it because they benefited directly from the organization?

Elite women supported their class in its rise to hegemony and took part in the creation of the new parliamentary monarchy. As such, their alliances were made with the colonial regime. They reminded the British, and their own men who were in the government, of their duty to those they ruled. In effect, they applied their nature/culture to resolve conflict and not to fuel it. Women were not to be found in the fight but in a position to resolve it. Their resistance often resulted in maintaining the status quo, thereby negatively affecting the lives of lower-class Egyptian women. Impoverishment as well as political and social immobility became the inheritance of the nonelite due to elite women's pursuit of power. Even elite women's resistance to the Muslim personal status laws, while having the effect of reminding their men of their duty, hurt females in the lower class. The extension of the harem to Egyptian society reduced nonelite women to subservience to their own men. Although ruling-class women wielded a great deal of power during this period and created a cross-class alliance, most of their activities helped to advance their own interests to the exclusion of the lower classes. Professional women initially consented to this alliance but, as the political and economic situation in Egypt declined in the late 1920s, this cross-class alliance of women began to break down.

4

Cross-Class Alliance

Managerial-Class Women's Uneasy Relationship with Ruling-Class Women

R uling-class women were successful in imposing their construct of woman on Egypt and in gaining the lower classes' acceptance of their hegemonic position in Egyptian civil society and control of the state. They accomplished this task through the promotion of cultural feminism that acknowledged essential separate spheres for men and women. By building on the tradition of the harem, which had become more bourgeoisified in the late nineteenth and early twentieth centuries, elite women left the private space of the harem to connect it to the wider international cultural feminist movement dominated by the West. This enabled them to extend their private woman's sphere from that space into public space in an attempt to domesticate both public space in Egypt and their men's privileged, secular, public sphere. Their domestication of Egyptian society helped to encourage self-regulatory practices among both men and women of the lower classes, adversely affecting nonelite women's position in public space. Finally, as their construct became part of the new state culture, it became synonymous with what it meant to be a good Egyptian.

Ruling-class women's success at achieving hegemony through the creation and implementation of their ideal of woman within the cultural feminist framework secured their position in Egyptian history as a progressive movement for all Egyptian females. This epistemological reorganization impacted lower-class women who could only receive the history of the hegemonic elite or an anthropological account of their local history.

In either case, nonelite women's response to the hegemony of elite women became impossible to analyze within this framework, which resulted in a view that lower-class females only acted as passive recipients of the hegemonic construct. As such, they remained confined to the margins of elite women's history or to their local history.

In order to reintegrate Egyptian lower-class women into the history of the period and to attempt to understand the complex dynamic that took place between elite and managerial women, it is necessary to investigate if there were oppositional constructs from women of the lower classes that may have weakened the hegemonic construct and, as a result, weakened the Egyptian state as a whole. If this were the case, then lower-class women did not merely consent to the hegemonic construct of woman, but they resisted it at the same time.[1]

Consensus for Egyptian women actually worked both ways. Ruling-class women sought cross-class alliance for a variety of reasons. New to public space, they began at a spatial disadvantage vis-à-vis lower-class women. In order for the elite to enter and control public space, they needed to make it like their domestic space. Employing their institutional feminism, they had to get nonelite women to give up control of that space or to accept the existence of separate spheres for men and women. Control for

1. Work of this kind continues with respect to Western women's history. See Karlsen 1987, where Karlsen refutes former analyses that attributed the end of witch hunts in North America and Europe to the dawn of the Enlightenment. Karlsen suggests instead that the persecuted women themselves (poor, widowed, non-Puritan, and nonwhite women) who were marginal to the hegemonic construct resisted their persecutors by accusing elite women of witchcraft. The magistrates refused to try the elite women and the hunt ended. Karlsen also attributes the end of the witch hunts to the development of self-regulatory practices among women, thus relieving the need for the state to exercise overt coercion, acknowledging the levels of women's consent to the new hegemony. Thereafter, marginalized women in this situation both consented to and resisted the new hegemonic construct of woman. Though I posit areas where ruling-class women agreed on general aspects of domestication, I am also aware that there were disagreements on certain issues between ruling-class women. Tafida 'Allam disagreed with Huda Sha'rawi over the issue of increasing the minimum age of marriage because she felt that it might dissuade young people from getting married (Ibrahim 1997, 138).

elite women, however, involved changing public space without them having to directly enter the public sphere.

Consequently, they needed the help of lower-class women, especially professionals, to mediate for them, both in public space and the public sphere. As a result, they found it necessary to ally with teachers, health-care workers, social workers, journalists, even entertainers. These women worked in professions that the elite could employ to advance their own interests. Since elite women did not work for a wage or desire to become professionals, they were reliant on professional women to actually implement their agenda in the public space they sought to remake and control. Therefore, consensus in this context should not be viewed as the ruling class having achieved success in generating self-regulatory practices among the lower classes that resulted in nonelite women just going along with the institutional feminist program.

The managerial class willingly consented to the elite's agenda. There were few disagreements over compulsory education for women or reforming the Muslim personal status laws. There was also agreement that British colonization had to end. The cross-class alliance of women in Egypt was strongest throughout the 1920s. Professional women also sought out the patronage of elite women to aid in the promotion of their own agendas, which secured this cross-class alliance. Conflict between the two groups appeared more over domestication issues, the kind of education women should be taught, the type of work women could or should do, and whether there really was such a thing as a culture of woman, a certain way all women act or should act. Here, professional women found it difficult to accept the cultural feminist framework. They could not influence the male, public sphere from their private woman's sphere as their relationship to public space/sphere had been historically less rigid than elite women's relationship to public space/sphere. Managerial women often had to work for a wage or desired to be associated with a profession that meant that their roles as housewife and mother were rarely separate from their professional roles.

With the coming of the Great Depression and the resultant economic problems in the 1930s, the economic and political divide between elite and professional women became wider, resulting in the breakdown of the previous cross-class alliance. Calls for social justice challenged the elite's attempts at performing philanthropic works. Managerial women opted for direct access to the public sphere of politics, including associations with extraparliamentary activities and organizations, or they attempted to collapse the Western conceptualizations of separate spheres entirely. This was in opposition to ruling-class women's attempts to persuade and feminize Egyptian politics through their alliances with Arab or Western feminists. Professional women were also not as concerned about pacifist means to accomplish their goals, reflecting their view that pacifism was not an innate female characteristic.

Culture also became an area of conflict through the 1920s into the 1930s. The elite women's use of morality as part of the cultural feminist agenda to get their men to be more responsible was matched by the professional women, who employed morality as a form of political opposition to the excesses of the Westernized ruling class as a whole. Finally, the elite's creation of a standard Arab state culture functioned to reify a romanticized view of Egypt and Egyptians that contributed to the marginalization of lower-class Egyptians, especially the peasantry, and negatively impacted Egyptian popular culture. Some managerial women responded by challenging this new state culture by providing alternative nonromantic constructs of Egypt and Egyptians of the period and by deliberately incorporating the *'ammiya* into their journals. Therefore, professional women took on only certain aspects of ruling-class women's agenda, and consensus seems to have started to break down in earnest by the 1930s.

With respect to the cross-class alliance of women, especially in the 1920s, professional women understood that they would gain from aspects of the elite women's platform, and they understood the power of ruling-class women—economically, politically, and socially—that would help them advance their own agendas. Elite and managerial women's interdependency cemented the cross-class alliance. Examples of consent to the hegemonic construct of woman and/or to the self-regulatory practices of elite women were evident in professional women's journals and memoirs. When Fatima al-Yusuf began her weekly journal *Ruz al-Yusuf* in 1926, she appealed for help from both Huda Sha'rawi and Safiya Zaghlul (known as Mother of the Egyptians), the wife of the Wafdist leader Sa'd Zaghlul:

I think that the Mother of the Egyptians had another opinion of me. When the magazine was begun as a popular culture magazine, I wrote a letter to both the Mother of the Egyptians and Huda Sha'rawi requesting their support of me and the Mother of the Egyptians did not reply. This inconsideration hurt me deeply. When the magazine became a political journal, the Mother of the Egyptians took the opportunity to write to me on some of the political issues, encouraging me and congratulating me. But I replied to her with silence also. I neither went to her nor did I meet with her. On the other hand, there was Huda Sha'rawi; she was quick to respond to me and she did not waiver from her encouragement and support of me. A bond of respect was forged between us. In one political encounter, we participated in a rough demonstration where we marched through the streets of Cairo. Huda Sha'rawi was at the head of the demonstration, marching on, shouting, giving it all she had. (1953, 107)

This account from Fatima al-Yusuf's memoirs is telling with respect to her consideration of her own womanhood and that of Huda Sha'rawi and Safiya Zaghlul. Safiya Zaghlul's snub of the journal *Ruz al-Yusuf* when the magazine dealt strictly with popular culture was considered a personal affront to its owner because al-Yusuf believed that the Mother of the Egyptians considered her to be a woman of ill repute. Al-Yusuf's perceived need to court not only the men of the Wafd but their women as well revealed both the power of these women as an extension of their men's power and the power of their construct of themselves as women.

As such, Fatima al-Yusuf was painfully aware that she was not one of these women and sought to forge a tie between them and herself, reflecting her desire to consent to their hegemonic image of womanhood. Through this consent, she wished to advance her own social position and that of her magazine. Whether her participation in a demonstration with Huda Sha'rawi, where Sha'rawi was in the front and al-Yusuf was in the rear, was a clear representation of a close relationship between them was not important. For al-Yusuf, it simply served as a means to legitimize herself and her journal as Egyptian in the hegemonic nationalist sense. The importance of this issue for al-Yusuf cannot be minimized because, though she was born in Lebanon, she did not come from the Egyptianized Levantine upper middle class. She came to Egypt as an impoverished adolescent and worked as an actress, representing the growing professional class.

Her consent promoted the elite women's construct as the hallmark of Egyptian womanhood and cemented the cross-class alliance between ruling class and managerial women in Egypt. Al-Yusuf continued to collude with elite women when she published accounts of ruling-class women's philanthropic contributions *(awqaf),* such as the one printed in the April 1, 1935, issue of *Ruz al-Yusuf.* Similarly, Sha'rawi's quick assistance to al-Yusuf also demonstrated a desire on the part of elite women to create an alliance, especially as they became increasingly dependent on professional women to access public space and the public sphere of discourse. Women such as al-Yusuf were gaining power in the area of Egyptian journalism. Sha'rawi understood the need for those of her milieu to reach out to professional women if they were to successfully implement their programs. The question that remains is why Safiya Zaghlul came around only after Huda Sha'rawi took the lead. Did the Mother of the Egyptians need to look to Sha'rawi as the model of a good Egyptian woman?

Yet Fatima al-Yusuf was not the only woman from this class or representing it who consented to the hegemonic construct. Labiba Ahmad, owner and editor-in-chief of *al-Nahda al-Nisa'iya,* exhibited her consent as well.[2] This was evident in an article in the January 1930 issue of that journal, which described Sha'rawi as the "greatest leader of the women's renaissance, not only in Egypt but in the entire East as well" and commended her support of Egyptian nationalism through her purchase of a sculpture created by Mukhtar.[3] The article wrapped up by asking for God's

2. See Fenoglio-Abd El Aal 1988 for a discussion of the transformation of *al-Nahda al-Nisa'iya* from the early 1920s until 1933. The magazine began as a supporter of elite women and the cultural feminist agenda but started to associate itself more with the professional class and urban poor, eventually becoming more Islamic in its orientation and more closely tied to the Muslim Brotherhood. See Baron 2005 (195–96) for a more extensive examination of this transformation. Baron specifically notes that Labiba Ahmad changed her title from *Hanim* (Lady) to *al-Hajja* (a title denoting that she had made the pilgrimage to Mecca) (212).

3. The Egyptian elite created its new state culture or nationalism around a romanticized notion of ancient Egypt and Egyptians. Mukhtar's sculpture "The Renaissance of Egypt," which featured the Sphinx, exemplified this idea.

blessings on Sha'rawi and on her beloved nation (9). The journal correctly acknowledged the power of Sha'rawi and her institutional feminism as integral to the national culture.

Though Ruza Antun Haddad was a socialist, she reached across class lines to acknowledge elite women's work in the field of health and sanitation. From 1921 to 1924, she partnered with her brother Farah Antun for her first journal, *al-Sayidat,* which featured many articles on domestic issues (Reid 1975, 97). In 1925, she joined her husband Nicola Haddad and created a new journal called *al-Sayidat wa al-Rijal*; it remained in publication until 1930. The latter journal was less concerned with domestic issues than the earlier one. However, in an article in the January 1929 issue of *al-Sayidat wa al-Rijal,* Haddad wrote that "the women are the ones who undertake the implementation of the directives on health issues in the matters of children, infants, national illnesses, epidemics, and other things. The women are the active helpers for health issues and their great projects" (213). Although she was aware of ruling-class women's ability to create self-regulatory practices among the lower classes through their control of health and sanitation issues, Haddad still acknowledged the importance of their work. She admonished the medical men in the article for not inviting the ladies of the elite to their professional affairs, especially since these women were in the forefront of the promotion of health issues. By praising the women for their efforts, Haddad appeared to consent to the cultural feminist ideal that women should influence the public male sphere from their private female sphere. Haddad, however, went further and attempted to bridge the separate spheres.

Munira Thabit also recognized the power of the new hegemonic construct of woman created by ruling-class women and its control by the Egyptian Feminist Union. She sought to court these women, if only, as Fatima al-Yusuf had done, to promote herself and her interests. Munira Thabit wrote in her *Mudhakkirat*: "If the Egyptian Feminist Union (which Her Ladyship Huda Hanim Sha'rawi founded under her leadership) had supported me from the first moment in my demand for the political rights of women, who knows where we would be today, certainly, not where we are now. The demand for rights pleads to be heard and increases in power with high society's wealth and influence" (1945, 38).

Clearly, Thabit understood the power of elite women and the Egyptian Feminist Union to create and maintain, through their work of domestication, a hegemonic construct of woman. She was also aware of their success at creating self-regulatory practices, so much so that she felt compelled to incorporate it into her memoirs (1945, 39). From 1923 to 1933, the Egyptian Feminist Union denied her a role in the organization and refused to implement her demands into the EFU's program, such as allowing women direct access to the public sphere as well as giving them the right to run for parliament.[4] Thabit continued to strive for the political rights of women through her work as a journalist and student of law.

She received a degree in French law in 1933, and the Egyptian Feminist Union invited her to a party honoring recent women graduates from Egyptian and European universities. For Thabit, it was the first time that she had the opportunity to enter the circle of the EFU and to attempt to push her issues from inside the organization (1945, 41–42). Like Fatima al-Yusuf, Thabit had to prove herself first, to garner the favor of the women of the ruling class. In this way, she attempted to consent to their construct of woman. Thabit could not ignore the power of ruling-class women in terms of wealth and influence. As with the other women who represented her class, Thabit understood that she had to acknowledge their construct of woman as well as the females who controlled it. In doing so, she consented to its reification as a reality, allowing for the women's further empowerment.

Nabawiya Musa early on was also a supporter of the elite's construct of woman and their attempts at domesticating all Egyptian women, as exemplified by her status as a founding member of the Egyptian Feminist Union.[5] Musa supported Huda Sha'rawi and elite women's insistence that

---

4. The EFU did not take notice of Thabit or her interests until the 1930s and, even then, did not seriously consider the implementation of her demands into the EFU's program.

5. See Rizk 2000 (11–12) where he discusses Nabawiya Musa's response to Munira Thabit as to what the EFU's agenda should and would be at the May 1923 International Women's Congress in Rome as the discursive battle took place in the journal *al-Ahram* in the two months leading up to the conference. Nabawiya Musa is in complete agreement with Huda Sha'rawi and the EFU. Sha'rawi and the EFU staunchly supported Musa's main interest, education for women, and denied Thabit's request to attend the conference and promote her agenda, suffrage and women's direct election to parliament.

Egyptian women needed to be educated before they entered the public/
political sphere directly (Rizk 2000, 12). Musa also countered Thabit's
insinuation that Sha'rawi was not committed to women's issues by citing
Sha'rawi's work in the various philanthropic organizations she founded
and supported. Like other managerial women, Musa understood the need
to reach across class lines to elite women in order to accomplish her specific goals with respect to education.

As a result of their inferior economic, political, and social position
in Egyptian society, professional women were often compelled to consent to ruling-class women's creation of the Egyptian woman as wife and
mother and to support their programs. However, their consent should
not be construed as an outright acceptance of that construct, as professional women could not be (as a result of their circumstances) or did not
desire to be the kind of woman that the elite were promoting. Although
they consented to the reified image of woman in Egypt, which contributed to its materialization, these women were actively involved in its
deconstruction through their creation of oppositional constructs. As a
result, women from the professional class or those who represented it
challenged the extension of the cult of domesticity to public space/sphere.
One way managerial women rejected the extension of the bourgeoisified
harem into the lower classes was through their insistence on being seen
as professional women, women who worked and who expected to receive
a wage in recognition.

They represented the first generation of women to engage in Egyptian
journalism, and they set the standard for the next generation of women,
including Amina al-Sa'id and Suhayr al-Qalamawy. (Both women would
enter the field after graduating from university.) Though Munira Thabit
earned a degree in French law after working as a journalist for several
years, neither Haddad, Ahmad, Musa, nor al-Yusuf attended university.
Fatima al-Yusuf did not even attend school; her troupe leader Aziz 'Id hired
a shaykh to teach her to read and write (Fuda 1972, 43). One could argue
that they were less professional women and more working women who
helped to create and to establish the profession of journalism. Their magazines were not an avocation or extension of their philanthropic activity as
was the case with ruling-class women. They did not remain marginal nor

downplay their participation in the profession like elite women. Instead, they promoted themselves and each other.

This was especially the case for Thabit and al-Yusuf, who had both worked before the creation of their publications and who competed against each other in promoting themselves and their journals.[6] Fatima al-Yusuf quit the stage in 1925 to start her weekly magazine (Le Gassick 1991, 443). *Ruz al-Yusuf* weekly began publication in 1926. Munira Thabit had written for other journals, including *al-Ahram* and *al-Balagh,* before she became the owner of her daily and weekly in 1925 (Thabit 1945, 21–22). Both al-Yusuf and Thabit saw journalism as an occupation and themselves as journalists. In May and June 1928, when Thabit was attending university in France, she left school to attend an international conference on journalism that was being held in Cologne, Germany; she went as a representative of Egyptian women's journalism (35).

Thabit and al-Yusuf were extremely competitive in the heated atmosphere of Egyptian journalism in the mid-1920s. Al-Yusuf named her weekly journal after her stage name, Ruz al-Yusuf, and the magazine covered stories about actors and actresses in Egyptian and Western theaters and cinema. Al-Yusuf became interested in changing the magazine to a political journal after the Sirdar Sir Oliver Lee Stack was assassinated and Sa'd Zaghlul was ousted from the premiership (al-Yusuf 1953, 104). At the time, Munira Thabit was considered the top woman journalist in Egypt, and her journal *al-Amal* was the mouthpiece of the Wafd (Abu al-Majd 1986, 196). This caused consternation to Fatima al-Yusuf, who found herself in competition with Thabit.

The competition boiled over on several occasions. Fatima al-Yusuf challenged *al-Musawwar* when the magazine ran a picture of Munira Thabit, calling her the first Egyptian woman journalist (al-Yusuf 1953, 104). *Al-Musawwar* refused to publish Fatima al-Yusuf's picture. On another occasion, Munira Thabit kicked around issues of *Ruz al-Yusuf* at the place where both of their journals were published. The incident upset Fatima al-Yusuf to the point that it elicited a promise from al-Yusuf's editor-in-chief,

---

6. Narratives of the lives of Fatima al-Yusuf and Munira Thabit can be found in Baron 2005 (177–88).

Muhammad al-Taba'i, to increase *Ruz al-Yusuf*'s market share enough to effectively kill Munira Thabit's *al-Amal* (Abu al-Majd 1986, 196). By 1930, *Ruz al-Yusuf* was the magazine of the Wafd, and Munira Thabit's *al-Amal* was out of print.

Managerial women did not see themselves as simply wives and mothers who were extending their private woman's sphere from their private space of the home to public space/sphere. They identified keenly with their roles as waged workers, professionals, and contributors to the development of journalism in Egypt. They challenged the narrow circumscription of ruling-class women's construct of woman as tied to a narrow biological definition. Professional women, never having been subjected to seclusion and veiling, did not accept a Western reorganization of the harem that was to be brought into public space to transform it and the public sphere.[7] They were already in both public space and the public sphere and sought to maintain, if not increase, their presence there more directly.[8] They reinforced this perspective of themselves as professionals when they acknowledged and promoted their colleagues' achievements.

In its February 1928 issue, Labiba Ahmad's journal *al-Nahda al-Nisa'iya* ran a picture of Munira Thabit with a caption that referred to her as a well-known journalist colleague whose success in university was proof of Egyptian women's progress and equality (49). Thabit entered the French Law School in Cairo in 1925 and left *al-Amal* in 1928 to finish her degree in France. Contrary to the description in *al-Nahda al-Nisa'iya* of Huda Sha'rawi as the leader of the women's renaissance, Thabit is described as a colleague in the field, revealing Ahmad's own vision of herself as a journalist. Thabit's success in university and career in journalism were her notable contributions to the women's movement. Here there appears to be

7. An example of the creation of a nationalist ideal of womanhood in India and the lower middle class's response to this ideal can be found in Chatterjee 1989. See Peter Gran 1996 for a discussion of the comparative nature of Italian Road states. Gran asserts that India and Egypt are both Italian Road states.

8. For Labiba Ahmad and the Islamists, spatial separation for men and women was essential while the Western concept of the dichotomy of spheres was blurred. In this paradigm, women do not need to enter public space to necessarily access the public sphere.

an acknowledgment that the movement in Egypt at this time was broader than the cultural feminism of the elite. In fact, Labiba Ahmad's contributions to the field of journalism are well documented. She hired many female apprentices to write for her journal; she also employed "the greatest number of female editors of any Egyptian magazine; from them emerged trailblazers in the Arab literary movement" (Khalifa 1973, 60).

In a March 6, 1926, article entitled "Miss Nabawiya Musa and the Minister of Education," Thabit's journal *al-Amal* took on the minister of education in defense of Nabawiya Musa, acknowledging "her capability in the significant works she had undertaken as a teacher, tutor, and director in the field of education" (11). It is interesting that Thabit would come to the defense of Musa, who only three years earlier had chided Thabit and her ideas on women's political participation as being too immature. Engaged directly in professions, Egyptian managerial women related to each other as professionals. Their public-sphere roles blurred with their roles in the private sphere, and their public-sphere activities could take place in public or private space.

In creating and maintaining their journals, Thabit and al-Yusuf had to compete for Wafdist support, especially in terms of advertising and subscriptions. This competition for economic support for their journals affected Thabit when *Ruz al-Yusuf* became the magazine of the Wafd and later affected Fatima al-Yusuf after she voluntarily split from the Wafd in 1935 (al-Yusuf 1953, 188). Unlike ruling-class women, managerial women did not have the luxury of unlimited resources for their publications.[9] They were, therefore, more directly responsible for their individual magazines and newspapers and for the promotion of the new field of Egyptian journalism in general. By directly entering a sphere that the elite had been actively attempting to reify as "male," al-Yusuf and Thabit courted a perspective that they were somehow aberrant women.

Thabit seemed to encourage this view of her by by promoting revolutionary, nonhegemonic ideas for women, including women's complete

9. See Baron 2005 (203) for a similar analysis of the difficulty of funding periodicals in Egypt. Baron states that Labiba Ahmad had financial difficulties with *al-Nahda al-Nisa'iya* in the early days of the journal.

equality with men in all aspects of life. An article entitled "Revolutionary Ideas," in the February 6, 1926, issue of *al-Amal,* described the backlash that the owner of the magazine received for challenging "the bitterness of unquestioning traditions and impeding customs" (8). As part of this backlash, European journalists nicknamed her the Amazon of the Egyptian Press (Thabit 1945, 25). On another occasion, Shaykh 'Abu al-Fadl al-Jizawi from al-Azhar charged her with deviance and ungodliness (al-Subki 1986, 71).

As an actress, Fatima al-Yusuf already had a questionable reputation that was far from the hegemonic construct of woman as housewife and mother. If she believed that her entrance into a more "legitimate" career as a journalist and owner of an Egyptian weekly and daily would change society's view of her as less aberrant, she was clearly mistaken. Fatima al-Yusuf stated in her memoirs how difficult it was for her journal to be taken seriously because, as she said, "it was still strange for an important political journal to carry the name of a woman and an actress" (al-Yusuf 1953, 107). Al-Yusuf confirmed this image of herself when she asked the esteemed literary critic, 'Abbas Mahmud al-'Aqqad, to join her daily. He initially declined the invitation to join *Ruz al-Yusuf* daily because he said that he did not write for a journal that carried the name of one woman. He later qualified the statement by saying he would not work for a journal that had one name, even if the name had been Sa'd Zaghlul. An offer of more money and benefits persuaded him to join *Ruz al-Yusuf* daily (156).

Nabawiya Musa also attempted to pursue her programs directly in the public sphere as chief inspector for the Ministry of Education. In this capacity, she called for educating girls in the same manner as boys and advocated for women to become principals. Women in teaching capacities represented an extension of women's roles in the process of socialization in public space. Women as principals or in positions of leadership were something else, apparently not congruent with the new nationalist construct.[10] The article entitled "Miss Nabawiya Musa and the Minister

10. See Gunther-Canada 2003 (37–71) for a discussion of the difference between Catherine Macauley's call for domestic education for women in her *Letters on Education* (1790) and Mary Wollstonecraft's call for a coed system of education that would

of Education," in the March 6, 1926, issue of *al-Amal,* defended Musa after she was fired from her position as chief inspector because of her insistence on bucking this hegemonic construct.

Ruza Antun Haddad, as a teacher and a journalist, was also among the pioneers who made professional work respectable for women; however, she and others had to deal with criticism from the Egyptian press (Reid 1990, 129). In all of these cases, Thabit, al-Yusuf, Musa, and Haddad came up against the elite's construct of woman but, instead of aiding its reification, acted to subvert it through their alternative subjective constructions of themselves as women involved directly in public space and in the public sphere. They, however, paid a price for doing so.

Managerial women, however, not only presented a challenge to the hegemonic construct of woman through the example of their own lives but also supported an alliance with other women who worked for a wage. A November 14, 1925, article in *al-Amal,* entitled "How Was *al-Amal* Received in the World of Egyptian Journalism," explored *al-Siyasa*'s reaction to Thabit's first issue and her program, which included getting Egyptian women to freely join men in education, intellectual life, and in high-ranking positions of work. The same article went on to explain that "in her pages did not flow a great number of men's pens" (12). Part of Thabit's project mirrored that of Labiba Ahmad, to provide opportunities for women to be trained in the profession of journalism. In an article in *al-Amal* dated September 25, 1926, Thabit also threw her support behind women teachers, arguing that they should be allowed to keep their jobs after marriage (4).

Similary, Fatima al-Yusuf wrote in her *Dhikrayat* about her attempts to help poor women find work during the Great Depression. She wrote, "I advertised about my need for fifty Egyptian girls to undertake the selling of *Ruz al-Yusuf* daily and weekly. In my visits to Paris it seemed most of

---

emphasize lessons in civic virtue in *Vindication of the Rights of Woman* (1792). Though supportive of the EFU's agenda, Musa favored Wollstonecraft's view of education, albeit in separate space, more strongly than that of Macauley. Dawson 2003 (111–31) discusses the struggle Louisa May Alcott endured writing her portrayals of ideal domestic life in her novels while living the life of a working woman.

the newspaper sellers were women and I wanted to open a door to respectable work to girls of my sort through which poor girls could work instead of begging, or gathering cigarette butts or doing domestic labor in houses" (1953, 170).[11] Instead of promoting jobs for women that were extensions of their roles as wives and mothers, Fatima al-Yusuf directly went out of her way to make sure that the women she hired would not only work for a wage (public sphere) but work in public space as well. She did not want women whom she identified with to be reduced to working as domestics in Egyptian houses where she felt women were much more in danger of being harassed or abused than in the streets. Ironically, she recounted that her plan was a failure due to the lack of support, stemming from the misconception that the female newspaper sellers would encounter more harassment from men on the street than they would in an Egyptian household. A caricature of this scene is pictured in al-Yusuf's memoirs (172).

Like al-Yusuf's and Thabit's support of waged women, Labiba Ahmad's journal *al-Nahda al-Nisa'iya* published an article in February 1930 entitled "Girl Amasses a Great Fortune by Her Wits." The author appealed to Egyptian girls to consider the article's portrait of woman as an alternative to that promoted by the Egyptian elite and cultural feminists. The article related the story of Anna Schreiber, a poor girl from Pennsylvania. Since her father could not adequately provide for the family, Anna, as the oldest daughter, was forced to go out to work. It is interesting to note that Anna eschewed domestic labor and instead headed off to New York, where she became a successful businesswoman with an office of her own. She then sent money back to her family in Pennsylvania (54–55). The choice to translate this particular story in Ahmad's journal—one where the heroine refuses to accept domestication in the productive sphere—is telling. It is also interesting that the journal would highlight a woman's success in

11. Al-Yusuf clearly influenced changing ideas about women in Egypt over the long term. Her editor-in-chief Muhammad al-Taba'i went on to hire Amina al-Sa'id when he left *Ruz al-Yusuf,* and al-Yusuf's son Ihsan 'Abd al-Quddus acknowledged his mother's influence on his creation of heroines and his concept of women in his writings (Murad 1980, 18).

work that was outside her innate abilities as a wife and mother, as defined by the ruling-class construct of woman.

Actually, from the first issue of *al-Nahda al-Nisa'iya,* published in 1921, Labiba Ahmad promoted the belief that women should learn business, engineering, nursing—a variety of skills generally reserved for men. In fact, she believed women should be trained for any profession where they could make a living as long as the profession did not adversely affect the raising of their children or cause the women dishonor (Ibrahim 1997, 99). She also supported initiatives to provide more money for teachers in Egypt (102).

In response to the *al-Ahram* poll, an article in *al-Nahda al-Nisa'iya,* dated April 1930 and entitled "Women Police," took on the same issue raised by the magazine *Ummahat al-Mustaqbal.* But where *Ummahat al-Mustaqbal* had argued that women were unsuited to police work as opposed to other forms of work such as teaching and social work, *al-Nahda al-Nisa'iya* took a different stance. The question was not whether a woman could do the job, the article argued, but of who would care for the home and raise the children if "we were to throw women into men's work in such capacities as education, medicine, law, and police work" (110). For Ahmad's journal there was no recognition of education as women's work and police work as men's work; all work that took place in public space was male and work that took place at home was female. As space was the organizing principle for Ahmad and the Islamists, men's and women's spheres were more blurred. The dichotomies of public/private spheres and church and state present in the Western epistemological tradition of positivism and romanticism were not present in the Islamist ideology. Following this, Labiba Ahmad rejected cultural feminism. The concern for her and her fellow Islamists was the effect that women working outside the home would have on the family.[12] The same issue remains a problem for working families today.

In another response to May Ziyada's poll on women police, begun on February 12, 1930 in *al-Ahram,* a woman who called herself Nadhifa Hanim

12. Fenoglio-Abd El Aal 1988 (75) cites a 1929 article of *al-Nahda al-Nisa'iya* (a translation of an article in the English newspaper *Sunday Express*) about the difficulties of married women in the workforce.

Hikmat presented a view on the subject that certainly did not fit Ziyadah's perspective or that of elite women and cultural feminism, for that matter. The woman in question claimed that she was willing to become a police officer if she could be paid a police colonel's salary and if she could investigate any criminal, male or female (Rizk 2002a, 5). The woman, who seemed to be satirizing the elite and their agenda of cleaning up vice, did not want to become a police officer for moral reasons or to become a better wife and mother as a result. She simply wanted to make a big salary and to wield control over both men and women in public space.

For women of the professional class, women's gender or culture was not defined by her biology. Nonelite women saw nothing reckless in the appeal for women police officers, which Tafida 'Allam's magazine expressed. Their argument was that women's innate abilities as wives and mothers did not determine whether they could handle men's jobs or would be better suited in positions that were extensions of their gender/sex according to the hegemonic construct. Other issues took precedence, instead, such as how much money a woman could make at a job and how much autonomy she would have. Problems arose that included issues such as who would take care of the home and the children if women worked (an issue ruling-class women apparently did not have to seriously consider since they could afford domestic labor). Furthermore, managerial women, unlike elite women, had to consider the question of women competing with men in a narrow job market during the Great Depression.

As a result, professional women opposed the cultural feminism of the ruling class and offered alternative constructs of woman simply by acknowledging that there was nothing natural about a woman's nature. As evidenced by these articles, they offered an alternative construct of the home, not as separate from the public sphere but very much a part of it. By challenging the cultural feminist construct of woman, professional women denied the existence of separate spheres for men and women and attempted to maintain their position in public space sphere or to collapse the separation of spheres entirely. In doing so, they sought to arrest the extension of the bourgeoisified harem to the lower classes that resulted in the domestication of women inside and outside of the home. Thus, they acknowledged their alliance with other waged workers, both men and women, in

Egyptian society. The alliance extended not only to the working class, but to the Egyptian peasantry as well.

An article entitled "The Catastrophe of the International Depression of Cotton and How to Remedy It," in the December 31, 1926, issue of *al-Sayidat wa al-Rijal* (the magazine owned by Ruza Antun Haddad and Nicola Haddad), emphasized managerial class concerns over the economic conditions that were oppressing the Egyptian peasantry. The article dealt with declining cotton prices adversely affecting the Egyptian economy that had become a monoculture by the early twentieth century. Various remedies were discussed in the article. One was forcing the United States to limit its production of cotton in order for the world price to increase, but the idea was rejected since the United States would only be one of a number of sources of cotton in the world (76–77).[13] Another remedy involved the idea of limiting cotton production and gearing up the land for fruit production (76–77). Unlike Ceza Nabarawi's cure for what ailed the Egyptian economy, published in the October 1930 issue of *L'Egyptienne*, which called for a continuity of Egypt's dependence on agriculture as it had been practiced for years coupled with new initiatives for commerce and industry, Ruza Haddad's journal instead argued for a social restructuring of the rural economy that would affect both the supremacy of the aristocracy and the upper middle class who depended on it.

It was a fact that the problem had more to do with land tenure and less to do with what to grow. The same article, subtitled "The Farmer Is Not the Owner," stated: "It is evident that the obstacle to growing fruit is not that fruit does not yield a marketable product if the farmer is patient. But that it lies in the fact that the owner of the land does not farm the land. The people here are of two types—one type owns the land, rents it and he is lazily having a good time in the cities spending and squandering the rent of his land" (76–77). The other type was, of course, the fellah (Egyptian

---

13. See Reid 1975 (118) for a discussion of Nicola Haddad's vision of socialism. Though not a revolutionary, Haddad's views incorporated the concept of class warfare, Marxism, something that Farah Antun's views had not. The results were evident in *al-Sayidat wa al-Rijal*, where Ruza Antun Haddad's perspective differed from her earlier views in *al-Sayidat*, the journal she shared with her brother Farah Antun.

peasant) who rented and farmed the land but did not own it. Haddad's journal supported the waged peasant against the landed aristocracy, especially with respect to workers' autonomy and wealth. It is interesting that the EFU's platform called for a diversification of crop production and an encouragement of industry but did not suggest any changes in land tenure (Fenoglio-Abd El Aal 1988, 144–45).

A similar treatment of the plight of the peasant can be found in a poem entitled "The Peasant and Cotton," in the October 27, 1937, issue of Nabawiya Musa's journal *al-Fatah,* in which the peasants expressed their desperation as a result of the collapse of the cotton economy (10). Musa, like Haddad, keenly empathized with the peasants' plight during the Great Depression. Labiba Ahmad also wrote about the collapse of the cotton industry, though she placed the blame on the West's dominance of the Egyptian economy (Ibrahim 1997, 101). Professional women accepted that peasant women already existed both in public space and in the public sphere and were concerned with the women's real-time situations in this space/sphere. Unlike ruling-class women, they were not concerned with simply offering charity as a means of domesticating working women but sought social justice means to improve waged women's position in the economic, public sphere whether it was to be found in public or private space.

What is also interesting is that managerial women had a realistic view of the peasantry as opposed to the romantic view of a time-encapsulated peasantry from the Pharaonic period. This notion included the idea that peasant women were more liberated than their ruling-class counterparts, a concept that fit the romanticist-based ideas of the cultural feminists.[14] An article entitled "Women in the Period of the Pharoahs," published in

14. Khalifa 1973 (57–58) discusses Levantine female journalists' proclivity for situating women in the Pharaonic period. Khalifa includes Balsam 'Abd al-Malik's journal *al-Mar'a al-Misriya* in this category. Though beginning in April 1927, Labiba Ahmad featured Mukhtar's sculpture on the cover of her magazine, the image was removed from the magazine in the 1930s (Baron 2005, 199). For a more complete examination of the discursive development of the Egyptian peasant as the timeless, authentic embodiment of the new Egyptian state who had not changed from the Pharaonic period, see Selim 2004 (85–86).

the November 1929 issue of *Fatat al-Sharq,* claimed "that women in Pharaonic Egypt were equal to men with respect to rights during this period," and that they engaged in "all forms of work including the watching of cattle, fetching water, basket weaving, tent weaving" (58)—activities that were physical and performed in public space. Elite women saw Egyptian peasant women as the most liberated because they had never historically been veiled nor secluded.

Ironically, while the construct of the Egyptian peasant woman aided in garnering consent for the state by creating an ethnogenesis and gender-genesis around the romantic construct of the Egyptian peasant and the peasant woman in particular, it did so through the cultural and intellectual exclusion of the peasantry as a historical phenomenon integrated into the social dynamic of Egypt at that time. Professional women's attempts at acknowledging the very real experiences of the peasantry surely impacted the aristocracy. It forced them to examine their complicity with respect to the peasants' historical situation. Although it may have been convenient for the aristocracy to accept a reified concept of the peasant woman as possessing an ideal life, the reality for peasant women during the 1920s and 1930s was something much different. Professional women acted to subvert directly the national, hegemonic construct of the peasantry and, in particular, of the peasant woman. Their actions threatened the ruling class's economic position and its control of the new state.

Another way that professional women challenged the hegemonic construct of woman as wife and mother was through a reexamination of the role of marriage. In an article entitled "The Conditions of the Social Systems" in the December 1928 issue of *Al-Sayidat wa al-Rijal,* the author questioned whether bachelorhood is a natural state of affairs for human beings and cited that it leads to segregation and the oppression of women in Egyptian society, concluding, however, that "of all the systems of equality and fairness, the institution of marriage continues to oppose the natural order in terms of carnal instinct" (75).[15]

---

15. See Reid 1975 (117), where he questions what Farah Antun thought about his sister's marriage to Nicola Haddad, the author of a book on love and marriage that Antun's journal *al-Jami'a,* had condemned as indecent.

In "Until When?" an article in the September 1932 issue of *al-Nahda al-Nisa'iya*, Labiba Ahmad wrote that "men these days are becoming more aware and they are all demanding that the wife not allow the adorning of herself to distract her from the responsibilities of marriage and also not from the matters of the home: they started looking at what we were doing as moral chaos with an eye of humiliation and scornfulness. They became so strong that marriage became a source of our social ills" (291).[16] Labiba Ahmad saw the connection between the ruling class's construct of woman that included the concept of women adorning themselves, often in clothes from the West, and its effect on marriage in Egypt. Ahmad herself had consented to advertising Western fashions in her journal. By 1932, she must have begun to realize that women's consent to the hegemonic construct of woman was causing a power struggle in marriage that men were using to their advantage. As a result, Ahmad, like the author in Haddad's journal, saw the negative impact that elite women's construct, with its consumerism and the related Western concepts of beauty, had on the self-regulation of women and on the institution of marriage itself in Egypt.

Since professional women saw the connection between the frivolous culture of the ruling class, rooted in Western consumerism, and its attempts at making the lower classes regulate themselves with respect to prostitution and drinking, they attacked elite women on this subject, often with satire. Thabit complained that the preoccupation of the Egyptian Feminist Union (EFU) with social reform and its development of self-regulatory practices diverted the group's attention from trying to gain political rights for all Egyptian women. She explained that, "actually the Egyptian Feminist Union had believed in these times that the

16. See Fenoglio-Abd El Aal 1988 (111) for excerpts from articles in *L'Egyptienne* and *Les droits de la femme* on the importance of women adorning themselves and maintaining their beauty. In one article cited by Fenoglio-Abd El Aal from a May 1930 issue of *L'Egyptienne*, the magazine touted the importance of sending Miss Egypt to an international beauty contest in Galveston, Texas, as Miss Egypt could serve as an ambassador, representing the best of her country.

Egyptian woman was not suitable for high rank or as a member of parliament. The group thought that it should depart from this subject and that it should direct its efforts to matters of social reform, the education of women, and their socialization" (Thabit 1945, 39). In "The Egyptian Woman and Destructive Extravagance," an article in the March 6, 1926, issue of *al-Amal,* Munira Thabit's magazine went further to examine the connection between Egyptian women's desire for Western fashions and the impoverishment of Egyptian families and the country as a whole (8). Where elite women promoted Western consumerism in their journals as a component of domesticity, Thabit's journal rightly saw its destructiveness for women and for Egypt as a nation. In fact, the article went so far as to claim that Western consumerism was turning Egypt, as a nation, into a prostitute (8). *Al-Amal* may have believed that ruling-class women's attempts at social reform with respect to curbing prostitution by targeting women prostitutes was misguided, as elite women's own consumerist culture was turning the whole nation into a prostitute.

In similar fashion, Ruza Haddad wrote an article, subtitled "The Demands of the Ladies," in the January 30, 1927, issue of *al-Sayidat wa al-Rijal,* where she humorously recounted elite women's demands for self-regulation:

> Madam L said: my proposal encompasses all of the proposals of women and men. The first thing I propose is to allow all women to carry a revolver and whenever an impertinent man opposes her, she gives him a bullet. I demand the closing of all of the cafes and the opening of clubs for men and women together. I demand the prohibition of all alcoholic beverages with no exception and the prohibition of the wagering of bets or no gambling because the games keep men from their homes. She said I demand the prohibition of smoking absolutely because I cannot stand the smell of tobacco smoke. (176–77)

In this article, Haddad not only conveyed the obvious attempts on the part of elite women to create self-regulatory practices but the power and privilege of elite women as well.

Though Labiba Ahmad supported the elite's self-regulatory agenda, including the prohibition of prostitution, she did so because vice was un-Islamic.[17] She did not relate prostitution to the capitulations or to the hygiene but, like Abul-Uyun, believed that it, like all vices, should be prohibited because Egypt was a Muslim nation. Though Munira Thabit and Labiba Ahmad may have come from different perspectives on the issue of vice in Egypt, they seemed to wind up at the same place. Western extravagance and consumerism fueled the desire for alcohol, smoking, and prostitution in Egypt. Neither Thabit nor Ahmad attacked vice to make their men more responsible to their women but because they realized that smoking, drinking, gambling, and prostitution were simply not congruent with the traditions of the nation.

The same theme was present in an article written in *Ruz al-Yusuf* in 1927 that was in response to an advertisement by a wealthy woman who had lost her dog and was offering fifteen pounds for the dog's return.[18] The author questioned how the woman could offer fifteen pounds for the return of a sick dog when so many people were in need. Concluding that the dog had committed suicide by drowning in the Nile, the author suggested that the woman was now free to send her fifteen pounds to an orphanage. Professional women received elite women's attempts at socializing public space and the public sphere by inducing self-regulation on the part of the lower classes with a degree of incredulity. They saw that the ruling-class women's economic and social activities contributed to the very problems they sought to reform. With wit and humor, professional women resisted the elite's attempts at self-regulation.

Their relationship to the hegemonic construct of woman, however, was convoluted. On issues that supported both classes of women, education for women and the reform of the Muslim personal status law, there was generally consensus. Acknowledging the power of ruling-class women, they sought to tap into that power in an effort to elevate their own social standing in the new Egyptian state and, possibly, to garner support for

17. Baron 2005 (201) discusses the religious basis for Ahmad's campaign against vice.

18. Kishtainy quotes from 'Abduh (1961) in Kishtainy 1985 (85–86).

their agendas as expressed in their journals. What they did not realize was that their consent to this construct, which they did not fully believe, had the effect of strengthening that construct and the state that relied upon it. As a result, on one level, these women consented to the break-down of their own constructs of what it meant to be Egyptian and what it meant to be a woman, thus aiding the reification of the ruling class's concepts of ethnicity and gender. Moreover, they aided the nationalist project as a whole.

Alternatively, managerial-class women actively resisted elite women's construct and domestication programs, challenging the elite cultural feminists' concept of separate spheres for men and women. Nonelite women did not share the same historical situation as ruling-class women as they had neither been veiled nor secluded. Their relationship to public space and the public sphere had been much more fluid. In order to maintain that fluidity, it would be necessary to halt elite women's attempts at reifying these spheres and marginalizing the lower classes. Some managerial women achieved this by continuing to work directly in public space and by working to increase women's economic opportunities in the public sphere. Others remained in private space with the spheres blurred.

Though they bore the brunt of society's scorn and fought many uphill battles, professional women continued to identify themselves subjectively as members of their professions, not as wives and mothers. This action and their support of each other with respect to professionalism directly worked to subvert the hegemonic construct of woman created by elite women. Their solidarity with each other was notable given the intensity of their competitiveness.

Alliances with their working class and peasant counterparts weakened the hegemonic construct and of the state that relied upon it. They promoted and supported women who performed waged work directly in public space and/or in jobs that were not extensions of the home. Concerns for the plight of the peasantry during the collapse of the cotton economy challenged the ruling classes' romantic view of the peasant as not part of the then-contemporary global economy or even as part of the then-contemporary Egyptian state. They countered elite women's philanthropy with calls for social justice. The managerial class recognized that women were suited to all forms of education and work. But it also raised the issue of who would undertake the unremunerated tasks performed by women, such as housework and the care of children, and addressed the problem of increased competition for jobs among men and women. By challenging elite women's promotion of issues of socialization and the development of self-regulatory practices, professional women sought to halt the extension of elite women's private sphere into the public sphere and advocated for women to work directly in public space/public sphere to advance their equality. Otherwise they collapsed the Western dichotomy of public/private spheres altogether. As the elite's construct of woman had become the nationalist ideal, managerial women's efforts worked to subvert the new Egyptian state.

5

The Hegemonic Construct of Woman

Managerial-Class Women's Resistance

F raming the history of the women's movement in Egypt in terms of
collusion and conflict may be new to the field of Middle East studies
but the model has been employed successfully with respect to work on
corporatism in Latin America and the rise of popular regimes.[1] This type
of framework is necessary to reveal women's complete activities, even if
they were not necessarily progressive for all women in the society. The
inability for postmodern feminists to acknowledge the collusion/conflict
model has resulted in a revival of the old positivist paradigm with narratives focused on structure and discourse, along with the narratives of
individuals. However, while providing much substantive information, this
approach fails to contextualize women's activities in the broader history
of the period.

The postmodern feminist perspective, then, leaves many questions
unresolved with respect to women's activities in the interwar period.
Did lower-class women simply collude with ruling-class women? If there
was conflict, was the lower class unified at all in its resistance? What was
the relationship of lower-class men to the ruling class and how did their
relationship affect their women? Were lower-class women responding to
the same issues as ruling-class women with respect to their men? These
are a few of the questions that have not been addressed by the dominant
paradigm.

---

1. Kicza 1993, Gutmann 2002, Garfield 2001, and Mallon 2000 employ the collusion/
conflict model in studies on Latin America.

As explained in the previous chapter, both professional- and ruling-class women became allied in the 1920s in order to more successfully implement their specific agendas. Their basic conflicts, however, remained with elite women attempting to influence the public space and sphere from their private home sphere, and managerial women continuing to either work directly in the public space and sphere or choosing to remain in private space with the spheres blurred. Professional women understood that their ability to attain greater access to jobs and higher positions was not only contingent on what went on in the economic realm but in the political and cultural realm as well.

The growing economic crisis and collapse of the cotton economy in the late 1920s and 1930s caused a growing rift between the ruling class and the lower classes in Egypt. The failure of liberal nationalism and the parliamentary system to successfully address the economic hardships of the lower classes caused professional women to rethink their relationship with the Wafd and parliamentary politics in general. Aside from the national economic crisis, managerial women also found that they were becoming marginalized from their own professions by the new standard state culture, which demanded they be trained to the new standards. Earlier they were able to enter the professions with little schooling and/or on-the-job training. Their ability to employ the new professions of teaching, social work, journalism and entertainment for their own social mobility began to decline by the mid-1920s. The previous differences between the two classes may have become more pronounced and led to the breakdown in the cross-class alliance of women, resulting in more conflict and the decline of Egyptian cultural feminism by the 1940s.

Consequently, professional women not only challenged the elite's hegemonic construct of woman economically but also politically and culturally. Eschewing the cultural feminist approach of influencing the public sphere from home, they fought to change the Egyptian government and parliament by advocating for women's direct participation in politics through parliamentary or extraparliamentary means. As they emphasized the link between the state and the colonial presence in Egypt, their resistance became increasingly more anti-Western and anti-imperialist. Although ruling-class women were more allied with the international cultural feminist movement, controlled by the West and with other Arab women in the 1930s, professional women remained more involved with political issues specific to Egypt. Finally, though elite women considered pacifism an innate quality of all women and allied with international pacifist movements, professional women were not above supporting direct means of resistance.

Culturally, professional women challenged the reification of the new state culture and its control by a select group of male intellectuals. If ruling-class women were impacted more by the Muslim personal status laws and directed their resistance toward getting their men to perform the same duties that they had to perform, professional women found themselves more marginalized by the new state culture that limited their ability to secure jobs without additional training. The marginalization extended to the *'ammiya* as a written medium of expression in the theater and in journalism, and had the effect of keeping less-educated women from these professions. Some professional women responded by continuing to feature the *'ammiya* in their journals. In almost all of the cases, however, they avoided the use of foreign languages, opting to employ Arabic instead. Additionally, unlike elite women who highlighted Western feminists' achievements or Egyptian women in the Pharaonic period, a period that the West accepts as part of its Western civilization, managerial women cited the achievements of Muslim women in the post-Pharaonic period. Through these means, they created an alternative discourse that challenged the ruling class's hegemonic construct of woman that elite women and intellectual men promoted.

Ruling-class women's journals including *Ummahat al-Mustaqbal, Les droits de la femme,* and *al-Mar'a al-Misriya* avoided the mention of politics and women's political participation as if women were outside of politics or considered politics a male preserve. *L'Egyptienne* did feature politics, initially Egyptian nationalist and later Arab nationalist.[2]

2. See Fenoglio-Abd El Aal 1988 (78, 82) for a discussion of the absence of politics in *Les droits de la femme* and *al-Mar'a al-Misriya.* See also al-Subki 1986 (114–15), where she notes that Tafida 'Allam did not really meddle in politics and took issue in her magazine *Ummahat al-Mustaqbal* with Huda Sha'rawi's political participation.

However, the magazines of professional women started as or became specifically political journals. The Wafd, and perhaps Sa'd Zaghlul personally, created Munira Thabit's magazine *al-Amal* as a mouthpiece for the Wafd's programs (Thabit 1945, 24). *Ruz al-Yusuf* was a popular culture journal before becoming a political monthly. Fatima al-Yusuf launched her daily in 1935. Reflecting the magazine's strong affiliation with the Wafd in the late 1920s, the oppositional Liberal Constitutional party dubbed the Wafd Ruz al-Yusuf's party. Mustafa al-Nahhas, the Wafd's leader, initially said that he had no problem with the name, though that would change later (al-Yusuf 1953, 122). *Al-Nahda al-Nisa'iya* also began as a woman's magazine and, by the early 1930s, became increasingly politically oriented toward the new *salafist* movements inspired by Rashid Rida and Hasan al-Banna. Similarly, by 1939 Nabawiya Musa's journal *al-Fatah* began to emphasize prewar politics over features about young women. Haddad's *al-Sayidat wa al-Rijal* was, from its inception in 1925 to its demise in 1930, politically connected with the Egyptian Left.

Even when ruling-class women's magazines, such as *L'Egyptienne*, dealt with political issues and the role of women in politics, the political perspective differed from that of managerial women. *L'Egyptienne* concerned itself with politics in general and did not take a specific political position (Fenoglio-Abd El Aal 1988, 82). Huda Sha'rawi believed that women could enter the political sphere only after they were established in their family and social life. She also sought the right to vote for elite women only (88). Munira Thabit, in contrast, had fought for the political rights of women for ten years before the EFU even began to consider it seriously. By attempting to include the demand for the right to vote for women in the Anglo-Egyptian Treaty in 1936, the EFU finally came around to Thabit's way of thinking. Thabit found it ironic how respectable the demand had become once it was sponsored by the EFU (Thabit 1945, 44–45).

Her explanation why Sha'rawi had waited so long to support the political rights of women was similarly interesting. Sha'rawi finally decided to agree with Thabit's demand for women's right to vote only after witnessing that Egyptian women had progressed to a sufficient degree to be considered intellectually equal to men (Thabit 1945, 50–51). Munira Thabit's efforts at earning a law degree in France, coupled with similar efforts by other women in the domain of education, waged professions, and politics, must have impressed Sha'rawi enough to change her mind. However, Thabit had envisioned a broader involvement for Egyptian women in politics from the creation of the new state in 1922, including women working in official government capacities with men (59–64).[3] She sought no limitations on Egyptian women's political involvement and questioned the EFU's unwillingness to accept women's direct participation with men in government positions.

In her attack on the Anglo-Egyptian Treaty, Fatima al-Yusuf revealed her perspective on Egyptian women's role in politics:

> The primary duties of woman at this stage is the consciousness of their rights and the obtaining of those rights, such as the right to vote in elections, the right to take up various government positions, the right to intellectual equality with men, and the right to appear beside men in social gatherings such as official state functions because the obtaining of these rights qualifies woman to execute her patriotic duties in a more apparent manner. (al-Subki 1986, 60)

Obviously, al-Yusuf did not consider her role as wife and mother to be primary, and her concept of a true Egyptian woman, in the nationalist sense, was quite different from what elite women were promoting.

It is clear that Munira Thabit and Fatima al-Yusuf sought a more inclusive role in politics for Egyptian women than did Huda Sha'rawi and ruling-class women in general. Only after acknowledging the strides

---

3. Munira Thabit imagined the possibility of becoming the prime minister, which revealed her perspective that women should play a direct role in politics in unlimited capacities. Also, see Rizk 2000 (11) for a discussion of an article Munira Thabit wrote to *al-Ahram* challenging the EFU's program for the Rome conference in 1923. Thabit was hurt by the men of the Constitutional Convention, who refused to draft a proposal to allow women to stand for membership in parliament, but she was even more hurt by the women of the EFU, who held a similar position that women should wait for direct participation in politics until they were better educated.

women had made in achieving intellectual equality with men, through the efforts of professional women, did Sha'rawi seriously consider demanding the right to vote for Egyptian women. Women's direct participation in politics was a different matter, however, as it implied an intrusion into the male sphere. With the right to vote, elite, educated women could employ their sphere as wives and mothers to influence the public sphere without directly entering it. Managerial-class women, though, were not interested in this means of political involvement alone and sought to enter the public, political sphere directly. In doing so, they subverted the separate spheres the institutional cultural feminists sought to maintain.

Another way these women rejected the ruling-class dichotomy that men engaged in politics and women influenced politics through their culture was evident in their early criticism of the Wafd and parliamentary politics and their support of extraparliamentary organizations, coupled with an increasing anti-Western and anti-imperialist stance. Though both al-Yusuf and Thabit were early supporters of the Wafd, by the early 1930s both women had begun to disassociate themselves from the party and from parliament in general. For Munira Thabit, the Wafd's inability to broaden the sphere of politics for Egyptian women and the party's link to British imperialism led Thabit back in the direction of the Egyptian Feminist Union, where she hoped she would have more success than in the past at incorporating her agenda into Huda Sha'rawi's organization (al-Subki, 72). Similarly, Fatima al-Yusuf became disenchanted with the Wafd after the fall of the Sidqi regime and the return of the Wafd under Mustafa al-Nahhas's leadership. She believed that the Wafd did not adequately pursue negotiations with Great Britain because of its obsessive duel with King Fuad (al-Yusuf 1953, 152).

Ruza Antun Haddad, with her husband Nicola Haddad, promoted socialism in their journal *al-Sayidat wa al-Rijal* (Reid 1975, 97). Nabawiya Musa, once a founding member of the EFU, became a staunch supporter of the palace. In "The Power of the Nation in its Unity," an article in the November 3, 1937, issue of *al-Fatah*, Musa called for the unity of the Egyptians under their king (4). Labida Ahmad also chose an extraparliamentary path through her support of the budding new *salafist* movements linked to Rashid Rida and Hasan al-Banna, the founder of the Muslim

Brotherhood.[4] In each of these cases, professional women became disillusioned with parliamentary politics and the Wafd. By the early 1930s, they took political positions that were developing directly in both public space and the public sphere. Their political involvement often took place outside of parliament as Egypt's civil society expanded. Unlike their elite counterparts, they were not satisfied with moralizing and socializing the male public sphere as part of their duties as wives and mothers. Like their relationship to economics, their relationship to politics was blurred, and their political responses were always more immediate and direct.

Though Huda Sha'rawi and the Egyptian Feminist Union engaged in politics (unlike Tafida 'Allam or Angelique Ghorayeb), it was still limited compared to the participation of managerial women. Huda Sha'rawi waited until after the signing of the Anglo-Egyptian Treaty in 1936 to take a firm oppositional stance against the Wafd (al-Subki 1986, 67). Part of her opposition involved Mustafa al-Nahhas's creation of an extraparliamentary, paramilitary organization called the Blue Shirts. The Wafd created the Blue Shirts in order to counteract the activities of other extraparliamentary organizations, especially the fascist Green Shirts of Misr al-Fatah, who were supporters of the king.[5] Sha'rawi decried their terrorist tactics, who carried out the Wafd's agenda to preserve democracy in Egypt.[6] As a pacifist, Sha'rawi

4. While Labiba Ahmad also supported the king, politically she believed that women should only be allowed to go out of the house to attend religious training, sermons, or the activities run by the Muslim Brotherhood (al-Subki 1986, 119). As these activities were not strictly religious but political in nature, Ahmad was supporting women's direct support for the *salafists'* social and political program in public space. Her view of the blurring of social and political spheres represented again Islamists' rejection of the dichotomy of spheres implicit in Western epistemology, including cultural feminism.

5. See Jankowski 1975 (18–19) for a discussion of the development of Misr al-Fatah, Young Egypt, the fascist youth organization founded by Ahmad Husayn in 1933. Misr al-Fatah created their own paramilitary organization called the Green Shirts, which clashed with the Wafd's Blue Shirts in 1936. Jankowski states that in the mid-1930s Misr al-Fatah was anti-Wafdist and pro palace, perhaps even receiving funding from the palace in the group's early years.

6. Wafdist students convened at the Congress of Wafdist Youth created a paramilitary organization called the Blue Shirts on January 5, 1936. Misr al-Fatah's Green Shirts

could not support the use of militarism by the Wafd in order to maintain a parliamentary system in Egypt. In fact, she did not take any of the writers associated with the extraparliamentary movements, including the Muslim Brotherhood and the Egyptian Left, seriously (68).

Conversely, managerial women jumped directly into the fray of the extraparliamentary activities and organizations that developed during this period. Nabawiya Musa, like Sha'rawi, sought the dissolution of the Blue Shirts but, unlike Sha'rawi, she did so because the king advised it. She thought that the organization could be better directed toward a unified nationalist goal under the king (al-Subki 1986, 69). As expressed in her journal *al-Fatah*, begun in 1937, Musa supported the palace, beginning each issue with a message about the king that she personally wrote. In an article dated December 10, 1938, Musa explained how she preferred a just dictatorship over parliamentary government, citing how dictatorships get things done while parliamentary systems do nothing (Ibrahim 1997, 152).[7] Muhammad Abu al-Isa'ad similarly explains that Musa wanted a government of the oligarchic minority and of the tyrannical autocratic palace (1994, 54).

Unlike elite women who continued to support parliamentary government indirectly, Musa seemed to be responding to the growing class inequalities and the parliamentary government's inability to change the status quo in Egypt by the late 1930s. Musa exemplified this concern in an article in *al-Fatah* dated August 10, 1939, when she fought the Majlis al-Shuyukh over the implementation of a stamp tax (Ibrahim 1997, 153). Another article, dated December 30, 1937, expressed not only Musa's understanding of the appeal of fascism, but also how dangerous the ideology was becoming:

---

were created in 1933. On July 9, 1936, both organizations were disarmed. Mustafa al-Nahhas returned official status to the Blue Shirts in December 1936, though they were forbidden to carry arms and parade in the streets.

7. See Jankowski 1975 (62–63) for a discussion of Misr al-Fatah's position that dictatorship was a better form of government than democracy. Musa's views on the subject parallel the perspective of Misr al-Fatah.

The United States of America became alarmed last week by the activity of the group the Ku Klux Klan as it appealed to fascist governments. This is the sad state which is breaking out in Europe and the American South these days and they are not aware of one of the predominant places when and where the fascination will take root next. Indeed, it proceeds from his neighbor's home and the emanations of his colleagues and of his countrymen who live in the adjacent streets appeals to him and there is one nation there and they do not see this critical situation in the confidence of their democratic government and this is the English nation. (15–16)

Though Nabawiya Musa admired aspects of fascism as an ideology, by the late 1930s she became disillusioned with the fascist experiments in Italy and Germany (Khalifa 1966, 208).[8]

Though also an early proponent of the Wafd, Labiba Ahmad decided to take a direct political position in her support for Islamic organizations, including the Muslim Brotherhood, beginning in the late 1920s.[9] Hasan al-Banna created the Muslim Brotherhood in 1928 as a religious and political organization opposed to the social and political failure of the liberal regime (al-Subki 1986, 117). The wives of the Muslim Brothers made up a women's organization called the Muslim Sisters in Isma'iliya, and Labiba Ahmad volunteered to head up a branch of the organization in Cairo (118).[10] Fatima al-Yusuf, for her part, supported the extraparliamentary activities of the students when she welcomed and promoted what she called the Revolution of 1935: when the students came out of Cairo University and demonstrated against the Tawfiq Nasim regime and demanded the return of the 1923 constitution (al-Yusuf 1953, 204–5). Four students were killed in the violence.

8. See Jankowski 1975 (58–59), where he states that Misr al-Fatah also became disillusioned with Hitler and Mussolini.

9. See Baron 2005 (209–10) for a discussion on Ahmad's association with Hasan al-Banna and the Muslim Brotherhood.

10. Unlike al-Subki's contention that Ahmad volunteered to be the leader of the Cairo branch of the organization, Baron states that Ahmad's association with the Sisters "remains unclear" (Baron 2005, 210).

In each of these cases, professional women took a specific political position that became increasingly anti-Wafdist and extraparliamentary. By the early 1930s, the contrast between the two classes became more evident. Unlike the passivity of ruling-class women, who felt that direct political involvement was either better left to men or could be influenced by women's peculiar abilities as wives and mothers, professional women actively subverted that construct. Through their direct involvement in extraparliamentary movements and by challenging the hegemonic construct of woman that this activity implied, they dismantled the Egyptian state. Though professional women took different paths to oppose the Egyptian state and its ruling class in the 1920s and 1930s, they were unified in their opposition to the hegemonic culture that supported it.

As a result of the breakdown in the cross-class alliance, elite women became more involved with international cultural feminist movements controlled by both the West and Arab women's movements in the 1930s as a means to challenge British colonialism in Egypt. Professional women remained focused on political issues directly related to British colonialism within Egypt. At the 1939 IAW conference in Copenhagen, Munira Thabit served with Huda Sha'rawi and Ceza Nabarawi as a delegate. Thabit's agenda, however, differed once again from that of her Egyptian sisters. She explained in her *Mudhakkirat* that Huda Sha'rawi called for world peace and the establishment of cooperation between Eastern and Western women; Ceza Nabarawi was concerned with the social deviation of Egyptian youth. Thabit explained:

> I insisted on dealing with the issue of the women's renaissance in Egypt and the demands of women and our hope of supporting the youth of today. My fanaticism and insistence on this choice was a subject of amiable jesting between Huda Hanim and Ceza Hanim. Huda Hanim cautioned me about this unruliness, advocating revolution, and to keep the treatment of this dear subject to myself and to modify it in a manner of peacefulness, moderation, and dignity and with a stipulation that it should not be inclined toward the language of revolution and the boisterous means which are being employed in Egypt. (1945, 67–68)

Thabit obviously had a different idea about what she wanted to accomplish at the conference than did the cultural feminists. She wished to broach the subject of the political rights of women, their direct political participation, and how these issues were tied to colonial politics and the extraparliamentary activities occurring in Egypt in the 1930s. Huda Sha'rawi and Ceza Nabarawi commanded her to temper her subject. Thabit promised to do just that but, like her other professional-class sisters, she was neither a pacifist nor a supporter of conflict resolution. With complete disregard for the other two women, Thabit scoffed at the League of Nations and took a swipe at the politics of colonialism (1945, 67–68).

Similarly, on the question of Palestine, Thabit supported Sha'rawi's call to classify Palestinian women as oppressed women in the same category as Jewish women under the Nazis. Thabit's view of the Palestinian situation was tied to the broader implications of the Mandate System and colonization in general (1945, 98–105). The focus of attention for Sha'rawi and Nabarawi at this conference was on cultural feminist issues and their association with colonial politics in general. Munira Thabit sought to employ the EFU and its influence in international and, in particular, Western venues to challenge Western imperialism and to promote women's direct political participation in Egypt. What she perhaps did not understand was that her demands and her adversarial manner remained contrary to the very framework of cultural feminism.

Like Thabit, Labiba Ahmad also exhibited an anti-imperialist and anti-Western orientation. In an article entitled "Our Daughters and Foreign Schools" in the August 1928 issue of *al-Nahda al-Nisa'iya,* the author questioned the effect of foreign schools on the social direction of Egyptian girls (256). This was not the first time the magazine had commented on the influence of Western institutions on young people in Egypt during this period.[11] Similarly, in the April 8, 1935, issue of *Ruz al-Yusuf,* an article attacked the son of Muhammad Mahmud for the disrespectful act of smoking a cigarette in front of his father. The magazine attributed his son's

---

11. See Khalifa 1973 (64) and Baron 2005 (199–200) for a discussion of Ahmad's more anti-Western focus in her journal.

behavior to the education he had received in England and his association with Westerners (26). Muhammad Mahmud was the leader of the Liberal Constitutionalist party, which was, aside from the king, the Wafd's main political rival.

In Nabawiya Musa's magazine *al-Fatah,* an article dated November 11, 1937, and entitled "Italy and Us" cited Egypt's lack of control over the positioning of troops on its Western border with Libya as the treaty government was obligated to support the Allies (8). The article went on to acknowledge that Egypt's fate was in the hands of mediators in Rome and London who did not seem to want to resolve the situation. Musa was acutely aware of the influence of Western colonial politics on Egypt, which left Egypt politically dependent on the West. She was aware of this at a time when elite women had developed a greater concern with politics in a more international setting tied to the West. In these examples, it is clear that the political direction of professional women was not only more anti-imperialist than ruling-class women but, more specifically, anti-Western as well.

While managerial women supported the boycotts and demonstrations of ruling-class women (an example of their cross-class alliance), they were not above taking a more active approach to politics, including their involvement in revolutionary activities and militancy. Munira Thabit's inclination toward revolution, demonstrated at the international women's conference in Copenhagen, attested to her desire to create conflict—not to resolve it. She said that she saw herself as a foot soldier, implying that, in her opinion, the conference was a battlefield with territory to be won (1945, 66). She did not feel, however, that she was an officer like Huda Sha'rawi and Ceza Nabarawi; her view in this regard probably contributed to her militancy.

Fatima al-Yusuf did not shrink from conflict either and actually encouraged the youth of Cairo to revolt. A November 26, 1934, article in *Ruz al-Yusuf* chronicled how the Cairene youth came to the publishing house to cheer the newspaper, its owner Fatima al-Yusuf, and the workers. She promised then and there that the paper would be in the forefront of the defense of Egypt and its rights until the very end (17). A year later, when the same youth put their lives on the line by challenging the Nasim government, Fatima al-Yusuf continued her support of the "Shababist" revolt. Labiba Ahmad was another example of a woman in the managerial class who did not see the female's role as strictly pacifist. In the January 1929 issue of her magazine *al-Nahda al-Nisa'iya,* an article discussed not only women's important role in the making of future soldiers but also in the making of future reproducers of soldiers. Ahmad's journal was acknowledging women's direct involvement in conflict, including armed conflict (1–2).[12]

Nabawiya Musa similarly admired military training and supported paramilitary organizations. She thought that the Blue Shirts of the Wafd could be employed to train Egyptian young men in military practices that could be used for a variety of social and patriotic objectives outside of politics (al-Subki 1986, 69). Unlike Huda Sha'rawi, Musa did not have a problem with the Blue Shirts because they were paramilitary. The problem with the organization, for Musa, was its participation in the realm of politics and, specifically, against the supporters of the king. Managerial women, then, did not consent to a hegemonic construct of woman as peaceful mediator of conflicts created by men in public space and the public sphere. Possibly their economic and political activities involved degrees of competition and survival that influenced their inability to be pacifist. Their militancy and support of extraparliamentary politics in Egypt during the late 1920s and into the 1930s challenged elite women's attempts at maintaining separate spheres for men and women in public space, securing managerial women's hold on that space.

Although they challenged the ruling class's control of the Egyptian state through their alternative means of political participation,

12. It is interesting to note that *al-Nahda al-Nisa'iya*'s editor Muhammad Sadiq 'Abd al-Rahman, in an article entitled "al-Ittihad al-Nisa'i" dated May 1932, agreed with the EFU on the issue of world peace. In fact, he agreed with the entire EFU platform except with respect to allowing women into public space. He seemed to pick those aspects of the EFU's program that would also fit the Islamist agenda. The question remains, however, as the Islamists became increasingly militant and political in the 1930s, did 'Abd al-Rahman's views for world peace only apply to women? What was the response of women Islamists to their men's consent to cultural feminism?

professional women attempted to resist the new state culture and their own men who controlled it. If ruling-class women saw the Muslim personal status law as their greatest obstacle, professional women had to contend with a state culture that not only included a hegemonic construct of woman that their own men supported, but also included a broader culture that acted to marginalize them from their own professions. Professional men, then, did not necessarily support their women in their attempts at maintaining a hold on public space in Egypt or gaining greater access to the public sphere. The men's alliance with the ruling class as state intellectuals often had deleterious effects on their women's professional status. Managerial women had to resist not only ruling-class women but also their own men's attempts at keeping them out of public space and decreasing their role in the public sphere.

Managerial women challenged this reification of a new state culture in several ways. Instead of highlighting elite Western women's accomplishments or acknowledging the timeless Pharaonic peasant woman as the hallmark of the nationalist ideal of womanhood, they looked to Egyptian women from the Islamic period as sources of inspiration. While resisting the employment of foreign languages in their journals and in other outlets, including education and the theater, and by calling for the employment of Arabic alone (either Classical or the *'ammiya*), they made a stand against the "third language" *fusha,* or Modern Standard Arabic. Its usage led to a standardization of the professions that resulted in the need for more formal training. For many lower-class women who could not secure this level of training, their path to the professions became blocked.

Nationalist intellectuals, who were overwhelmingly male, began to create and reify a new state culture in the late nineteenth century. They included early on the disciples of Muhammad 'Abduh, Qasim Amin and 'Abdallah al-Nadim, and later, Muhammad Husayn Haykal, Tawfiq al-Hakim, Taha Husayn, Mahmud Taymur, and 'Abbas al-'Aqqad. According to Stephen Sheehi, "Arab intellectuals agreed that the native Arabo-Islamic culture was in a state of 'decay' and, consequently, in need of infusion of positivist knowledge" (1999, 1). Samah Selim goes on to explain that "their desire to reform society was shaped by the scientific disciplines and intellectual discourses of an imperial, racialist European epistemology that essentialized the Orient as its corrupted other. It was also shaped by their very real political and economic interests as a ruling class" (2004, 88).

Professional men allied with both men and women of the ruling class in their acceptance of a Western epistemology that acknowledged separate spheres: for the elite and the peasantry, and for men and women. Their writings contributed to the reification of a discourse that promoted the Egyptian peasant from the Pharaonic period as the authentic, nationalist model (Selim 2004, 86). Ruling-class women, who accepted the dichotomy of separate spheres for the genders, also consented to this construct of the Egyptian peasant woman and included it in their own journals.[13] With this discursive treatment, the *fellah* and Egyptian women in general became relegated to a static, cultural sphere, outside of economics and politics. Once there, they could only affect economics and politics from their cultural domain. Their marginalization in this way effectively excluded them from incorporation into the nation's history.

Ruling-class women accepted their marginalization and responded to their men's Social Darwinism by resorting to a romanticist cultural feminism. Professional women once again took the direct approach by opting to challenge the Western paradigm head on and incorporating the contributions of Arab/Islamic women in their writings over Western women and/or Egyptian women from the Pharaonic period. At the very least, they acknowledged the importance of a nonsecular form of Islam in their own lives. Managerial women saw nothing deficient in the Arab-Islamic heritage and challenged both ruling-class men's positivism and elite women's romanticism.

For the ruling class, Muslim Egyptian women from the past did not fit the model of the new Egyptian state that they were in the process of constructing. This selective heritage-oriented approach differed significantly from that of professional-class women whose concept of the good old days paralleled the *salafism* of ruling-class women. Where the elite employed the reformist Islam of Muhammad 'Abduh to resist the duties their men

13. See Badran 1995 (145) for examples of the use of Pharaonism by elite women to support women's rights to education.

placed on them through the imposition of the Muslim personal status law, professional women sought a more authentic *salafism* that was devoid of European influence.

As the Western heritage model severs the West's connection to Egypt in 639 C.E., there could be nothing definitively Western about professional women's connection to a post-Pharaonic, Islamic Egypt in heritage terms. Consequently, though both classes sought to reconstruct their heritages, ruling-class women accepted the Pharaonic model and its connection to Western civilization. Managerial women chose the Islamic heritage model, though it was rejected by the West. The construction or deconstruction of the Egyptian state depended on a reified heritage of what it meant to be Egyptian. Though the construction of heritage is ahistorical and presentist, modern nation-states rely on a reified construct of heritage for nationalist purposes. For women of this time, alternative constructions of heritage became another area of conflict over what the new Egyptian woman, in nationalist terms, was to be. What is interesting is that the conflict reveals just how important such gender constructions are to the creation and maintenance of states in real political terms.

One example of the reconstruction of the Arab/Islamic heritage can be found in an article entitled "The Rise of Women in the East," in the August 1928 issue of *al-Nahda al-Nisa'iya,* where the achievements of women such as Aisha and Zaynab were employed as models for Egyptian females (256). Munira Thabit exhibited a similar concept of heritage as Labiba Ahmad when she sent a petition in March 1927 to the legislative and executive branches of the Egyptian government and to the media, demanding the political rights of women:

> The Islamic religion was the first antecedent to this equality for it gave women judicial freedom without permission from their husbands and the freedom to conduct business in all capacities from buying and selling, lending and borrowing to leasing and taking a lease and philanthropy and other things. And the jurisprudents acknowledged that women also had the right of the administration of justice and the administration of the affairs of the congregation. (Thabit 1945, 31–32)

Thabit acknowledged that many women ruled during the Islamic period, including Shajara al-Durr (Thabit 1945, 32).

Like Ahmad, Thabit drew on Islamic tradition as a means of constructing a new heritage for Egyptian women, perhaps a more authentic heritage that was devoid of Western connections. Fatima al-Yusuf herself was raised a Muslim, converted to Christianity, and chose to reconvert to Islam later in her life. Her social conscience directed her journal toward the forefront of defending the downtrodden in Egypt (Kishtainy 1985, 80). To this effect, the articles in both her daily and weekly publications often appealed to God for justice. For Nabawiya Musa, *al-Fatah* was dedicated first to Allah and then to the king (Ibrahim 1997, 150). Aside from Ruza Haddad, the remainder of the managerial women openly incorporated references to God, the Islamic heritage, and Islamic women into their journals. They increasingly turned from the West in their search for an authentic heritage and female role models to reconnect with their Islamic past. They employed this reconstruction to challenge the hegemonic construct of a timeless Egyptian woman from the Pharaonic period linked discursively to modern Western women. In this way, professional women also resisted men of their class and their alliance with the elite with respect to the creation of this discourse. Their attempts to undermine the new state culture led to the essential subversion of the state.

If one accepts that culture is transmitted through language and made real through written discourse, then the language that Egyptian women chose to transmit their ideas also reflected their class positions. Where ruling-class women used Western languages (especially French) and Arabic (without the inclusion of the *'ammiya*) as the medium for their journals, managerial women generally only employed Arabic with the inclusion of the Egyptian *'ammiya* into their writings and supported its use in other forms of literature.[14] An article in the February 7, 1938, issue of *al-Risala* questioned the seriousness of women journalists who wrote in foreign languages and who possessed little knowledge of their own language and

---

14. Munira Thabit did have two journals beginning in 1925, *L'Espoir*, which was in French, and *al-Amal*, which was in Arabic. All of the other managerial-class journals were in Arabic.

history, doubting whether their libraries even contained the work of a Middle Eastern author.

The fear that Arabic was giving way to Western languages in Egypt or was being Europeanized in some sense was a theme common to all of the managerial women. Niloofar Haeri discusses how *fusha* became separate from Classical Arabic and its connection to Islam, leading to a secularization of the language that paralleled the secularization of Islam at the time (2003, 47). ʿAbd al-ʿAlim al-Qabaʾni notes that while there was great interest in the late nineteenth century in creating Arab journalism, there were concerns over the Europeanization of the language and the inability for all "Arabs" to understand the *fusha* (1973, 100). Managerial women expressed similar concerns over the loss of Arabic due to the incursion of Western languages and the Europeanization or Westernization of the language in the creation of the "third language."

In an article entitled "Our Daughters and Foreign Schools," in the August 1928 issue of *al-Nahda al-Nisaʾiya*, the author questioned whether foreign schools were consistent with the Egyptian way of life and concluded that the "female students learn in them [foreign schools] Western languages and very little Arabic" (256). Labiba Ahmad, seeing that the new nationalist culture had a strong Western influence, sought what she believed was a more authentic Egyptian culture transmitted through Arabic. With respect to foreign schools and their influence on Egyptian girls, Nabawiya Musa criticized the teaching of foreign languages and the neglect of the national language (Abu al-Isaʿad 1994, 99). Musa, like Ahmad, feared the influence that Western languages were having on Egyptian youth and on the future of the national culture.

The marginalization of Arabic in favor of Western languages and the Westernization of Arabic with the creation of the *fusha* also had real implications for managerial women. In the late nineteenth and early twentieth century, the ability for amateurs to enter the professions in Egypt and to be trained on the job increased. This situation was especially evident in the theater. As the satirical press employed actors and actresses from the theater, a similar effect occurred in the field of journalism. The number of actresses, especially Muslim ones, grew precipitously after the First World War (Landau 1958, 76). The majority of these women had no formal training but could enter the profession because the *'ammiya* was employed in the theater and the satirical press.

One such woman was Fatima Rushdi, who "had no foreign training and spoke only Arabic; she played for the masses." Rushdi started her own theatrical troupe in 1926, but her most successful plays "were rendered in colloquial Arabic" (Landau 1958, 81). Egyptian light theater, which employed the *'ammiya,* became more popular after World War I and provided opportunities for women who were not formally trained in the profession or in foreign languages to enter the theater to become actresses, dancers, and singers. Fatima al-Yusuf employed the stage as a springboard for her entrance into journalism. Though not an actress, Nabawiya Musa was also able to become chief inspector of schools without formal training for the position.

The ability for Egyptian women such as Musa, Thabit, al-Yusuf, Haddad, Ahmad, Rushdi, and Umm Kulthum to work within their respective professions and to influence their direction without formal training at this time was significant. The democratization of the professions in Egypt did not last long, however, and with the creation of a standard state culture transmitted in a standard language, *fusha,* women found it much more difficult to enter or to maintain their positions within these professions by the mid-1920s. Specifically with respect to the standardization of the theater profession, actors and actresses became true professionals, limiting the ability for amateurs to try their luck on the stage and learn their craft on the job (Landau 1958, 105).

The new professionals in the theater specialized in one area, such as acting or singing, and were forced to go to Europe and the United States to hone their skill. Actors and actresses who could not go abroad had to attend the High Institute of Dramatic Art (Landau 1958, 105). As troupes visited other Arab countries, pan-Arab cultural connections won out over Egyptian national culture (106). Finally, as the government began to fund the advancement of Arab theater, plays written in the *'ammiya* were banned from government-sponsored competition by 1932 (91). Ibrahim 'Abduh describes a similar development when the Egyptian press began to feature Arabic poetry and literature, along with research in the arts and sciences, in Arabic *(fusha),* creating a tension between *fusha* and the "living languages" that the journalists had to work out (1982, 223).

Parallel developments can be found in the field of education, especially with the opening of higher education to women in Egypt in 1929, leaving only those who could secure this level of education or formal training in the *fusha* able to access the professions. Women who could not be professionally trained and/or could not work within the new state culture with *fusha* as its medium found the gates to social mobility closed. They challenged men in the professions with respect to their involvement in the creation of the state culture and its medium, *fusha*. They accomplished this by deliberately employing the *'ammiya* in their discourse. Though writing in the vernacular may be a nonissue in the West, in the Middle East, and especially in Egypt, it remains a source of contention.[15] The *'ammiya* was a constant presence in Fatima al-Yusuf's articles and, of course, in the political cartoons. In an article in *Ruz al-Yusuf* dated November 18, 1935, the author addressed the issue of employing the *fusha* in the theater:

> It is for all the world to see that the Arabic language does not lend itself to the theater and it is a sign that no one knows how to speak the language except in the *'ammiya*. It is necessary to insist that the [Arabic] language be changed into the *'ammiya* in all of the plays that were distributed among the acting troupes and to inform the men of belle lettres, at whose head are Taha Husayn and Tawfiq al-Hakim to set free Arabic if they want their stories and plays to be successful. (36)[16]

Fatima al-Yusuf supported light theater against the newer, more professional plays that were being written. Her actions represented a cultural opposition to the new state culture but, more practically, helped actresses on the stage to keep their jobs (al-Yusuf 1953, 65). Maintaining women in the professions was important because famous actresses and singers, such

15. Haeri 2003 discusses the continued difficulties in incorporating the Egyptian vernacular into the written word. Some scholars consider the *'ammiya* to be a colloquial, rather than a vernacular language. As everyone in Egypt speaks the *'ammiya*, I refer to it as the Egyptian vernacular.

16. See Allen 2000 (193–215) for a discussion of the problems associated with the various languages employed in Egyptian theater in the early twentieth century, especially with respect to the playwright Tawfiq al-Hakim.

as Umm Kulthum, often employed their professional fame to support economic and political activities—just as Fatima al-Yusuf had done.[17] Al-Yusuf made great contributions to the development of the satirical press in Egypt. The use of the *'ammiya* in her daily and weekly was closely tied to the popular poetic form *zajal* and Egyptian theater. In the satirical press, these artistic forms intersected; she added another artistic form, the political cartoon, with captions also in the *'ammiya*. Her most popular cartoon character was al-Misri Effendi, an Egyptian (professional) everyman, created in 1932.[18]

The subjective decision on the part of the professional class to communicate in the *'ammiya* was as much a political response as it was an artistic one. Khalid Kishtainy rightly explains that its use was an attack on imperialism (1985, 99).[19]

Marilyn Booth goes further to show that:

In the 1920s, *zajal* may have benefited from the growing interest among "mainstream" writers in dialect as a language of literary realism, an expression of cultural nationalism, and, for some, an articulation of Egyptian separatism based on pride in Egypt's unique heritage. The demands of a national literature that would articulate Egyptian experience might well embrace the use of the Egyptian tongue. Dialect's greater acceptability as an artistic language, however momentary, may have been one factor in broadening the media context for *zajal* publication from the satirical press outward; around 1930, *zajal* began to invade other sectors of the press. But at the same time, *zajal* continued to be an art apart, and this was one of its political strengths. Notably, the emerging labor-oriented press could embrace it as a non-elite form

17. See Abu al-Majd 1986 (194) for how Umm Kulthum paid four pounds for one copy of *Ruz al-Yusuf* weekly when Fatima al-Yusuf and her editor Muhammad al-Taba'i went to her apartment to sell subscriptions for the new journal. A year's subscription was forty piasters.

18. Kishtainy 1985 (80–81) states that Muhammad al-Taba'i and Sarukhian created the political cartoon al-Misr Effendi. Fatima al-Yusuf claimed that she came up with the idea.

19. See Kishtainy 1985 (183–84) for a discussion of how the Egyptian government banned the use of the *'ammiya* to transmit political issues in the press in the late nineteenth century.

perfectly suited to expressing workers' class solidarity and voicing their demands. (1992, 433)[20]

Nabawiya Musa incorporated the *'ammiya* into her journal *al-Fatah*.[21] Both Fatima al-Yusuf and Munira Thabit employed the *'ammiya* in their memoirs.

For professional women, then, the use of either Classical Arabic linked to Islam and/or the *'ammiya* challenged the growing Europeanization and secularization of the Arabic language as a national medium for the transmission of a new Egyptian state culture. Their choice of a language for their discourse paralleled their idea of an Egyptian heritage that was separate from the West and Arab nationalism, evidenced by the post-Pharaonic, Egyptian Muslim women they chose as role models. Through these means, professional women created an oppositional culture that they employed to resist the culture of the ruling class and professional men.

Unlike professional men and the ruling class, managerial women did not accept the dichotomy of men's and women's spheres implicit in the Western positivist/romanticist epistemology. They could not work from the premise that they could influence the social and political public male sphere from their female sphere as wives and mothers because they did not acknowledge that a woman's sphere, or a peasant's sphere for that matter, was innate and organic. As such, they were forced to challenge their political and social marginalization directly. In this way, they attempted to maintain their hold on public space and sphere. For women such as Labiba Ahmad, they deconstructed the epistemological spheres entirely, holding on to their place in the public sphere while occupying private space. Because the hegemonic state culture was closely tied to the West, substantively and epistemologically, managerial women's resistance became more anti-Western and anti-imperialist.

20. Booth also explains in the article that the use of the *'ammiya* in print allowed more people to get the information since the vernacular was more easily translated by word of mouth for the nonliterary than the *fusha*.

21. The poem entitled "Al-Fallah wa-l-Qutn," printed in the October 1937 issue of *al-Fatah*, was written in the vernacular.

As with their attempts to challenge the creation of a hegemonic state culture that was not authentically Egyptian, managerial women did not look outward toward alliances with other Arab women or with cultural feminists in an international context. Instead, they focused directly on the political situation as it was developing in Egypt. Their response to the deteriorating economic and political conditions was direct. Some of the women actively sought government positions for women in parliament and the ministries. They all supported extraparliamentary activities and organizations. As their politics often required rivalry and competition, and sometimes revolution, they rejected the hegemonic construct of woman as innately pacifist and bent on conflict resolution. Their activities had the effect of not only dismantling the cross-class alliance of women that had been in effect since the 1919 revolution but undermined the new Egyptian state as well. After 1939, both parliamentary politics and cultural feminism in Egypt would be in decline.

6

Summary

Orientalism as a methodological framework for the study of Egyptian women continues and is exemplified in terms of political and cultural structures, including nationalism, gender, ethnicity, language, and religion. Attempts by symbolic anthropologists, developmentalists, neohermeneutic and poststructuralist scholars have often led only to a reorganization of the Orientalist paradigm. This paradigm focuses on the genealogy of social and political structures, as if the structures were the subjects with women marginally related to them. They appear to influence the women but not the other way around. In some works, the structures undergo change; in other works they do not. In either case, Egyptian women remain marginalized because their subjective role in the creation, maintenance, and subversion of the social and political structures is rarely discussed. Their position is always one of oppression. It is as if they must wait for some mechanism, usually from the West, to free them.

This analysis relieves Egyptian women from any complicity in their oppression and, at the same time, removes them from a broader incorporation into history. Perhaps this is due to a continued reliance on positivism as a framework for history even in the new postmodern studies, which still draw on the Eurocentric Oriental Despotism model where Western women are more progressive than those of the Middle East. So it stands to reason that a group of Westernized women in Egypt would be able to move the female population forward better than women representing anti-Western perspectives, regardless of whether the facts (essentialism) support that reason. Another problem rests specifically with Women's Studies, which developed a paradigm of gender as a category of analysis to fit the period of the cross-class alliance of women and has not rethought this framework of analysis in the current divisive, neoliberal period. Since this does not fit women's history currently, it suggests that not just collusion exists between women, but conflict as well.

Liberal Enlightenment and cultural feminism were part of the great discursive tradition of the eighteenth century. Before this time, discourses stipulating who and what women were or were to be did not exist; nor did effective means of transmitting the discourse exist to make the concept real. Modern nation-states that needed to rely on sophisticated means of state culture to get people to consent to the legitimacy of the elite's rule were not present. Global capitalism had yet to cause the great divisions in wealth nationally or internationally. From a historical viewpoint, it would seem that getting a consensus among women on what the nature of their gender should be was probably impossible before the eighteenth century. Women's multiple concepts of themselves as women that existed before this period could not have mechanistically disappeared with time.

As nation-states developed within the context of global capitalism, ruling classes employed the discursive traditions of the eighteenth century, including feminism, to their advantage. Cultural feminism particularly, which challenged Liberal Enlightenment feminism, followed Jean-Jacques Rousseau and acknowledged a reified woman's sphere based on her nature as wife and mother. Women were confined to this social sphere and could not enter the political and economic sphere of men; they could, however, use their nature to feminize the male sphere. Cultural feminism probably emerged as the most dominate form of feminism by the late nineteenth century and fit the period of developing nationalisms in the world. Within nascent and developed nation-states whose ruling classes had not become international yet, this form of feminism helped to create cross-class alliance among women, generating gendergenesis, a consensus to a national construct of woman. Gendergenesis became part of the broader ethnogenesis, or nationalism, that nation-states employed to garner consent from the masses to the ruling class. However, collusion and consensus did not displace conflict. During periods of crisis, women, especially from the lower classes, created alternative concepts of themselves. They attempted to reify those concepts in opposition to the unified hegemonic gender of the state and the institutional feminism that had created it.

This book challenges both positivist and postmodernist views that women always acted in a progressive manner in history. It questions the contention of Women's Studies (now Gender Studies) that gender can be employed as a framework of analysis. Feminists and gender-studies scholars have been sensitive to negative portrayals of women in history. To understand the history of women as presented in this study is to acknowledge that they do not always act progressively in history but they do, indeed, act; any removal of their activities from history does not benefit them. This approach is especially important to the history of Egyptian women who bear not only the burden of Orientalism but Western feminism, too. Understanding women's complex relationship to power—economic, political, cultural, and epistemological—is essential. Women do not only work for advancement for themselves and other women, but they also create and maintain forms of oppression for themselves and other women.

Specifically, this study seeks to understand the indigenous dynamic involving women of the Egyptian landed aristocracy with the Levantine/European and Egyptian upper middle class and their creation of a discourse of feminism that became institutionalized in the newly created Egyptian state culture. Their desire to directly enter public space after 1919 required that they gain control of it from women who were already occupying it. Like aristocratic *salonnière* women in eighteenth-century France, aristocratic women, with their upper-middle-class counterparts in Egypt, initially attempted to influence the public space/sphere from their salons. In them, elite Egyptian women entertained professional men who shared their liberal positivist views. The women, however, accepted only the views that supported their own class interests.[1] Here the women looked to the Social Darwinist reformers 'Abduh, al-Nadim, and Amin to provide them with a road map for the philanthropic activities that they would perform

---

1. See Pekacz 1997 (405–14) for a discussion of the *salonnières'* preference for French opera over the *philosophes's* preference for Italian opera. Though the *salonnières* provided the forum for the *philosophes* to advance their taste and to promote their new concepts of French nationalism, they remained loyal to their class and its views on what constituted a true nationalist in France.

in public space. They also courted state intellectuals Husayn, Haykal, and Taymur to create a state culture that would support their agenda.

However, Egyptian ruling-class women always possessed, even in the harem, a degree of (public sphere) economic and political power that *salonnière* women in eighteenth-century France never had, and they could have opted to remain where they were. But the same professional, reform-ist, male intellectuals that the elite women entertained saw the harem as an anachronism that was partly responsible for the decay of Oriental civi-lization. With male intellectuals' call to bourgeoisify the harem, women prepared to enter public space directly, though they had no intention of entering the male, public sphere of politics and waged employment. They took the opportunity of the 1919 revolution to make their move.

Their entrance coincided with the development of a new ruling class in Egypt, comprised of the landed aristocracy in alliance with the Egyptian-ized Levantine/European and native Egyptian upper middle class. This alliance allowed the aristocracy to move toward capitalist investment in commerce and industry, which was controlled by the upper middle class. By maintaining feudal conditions, especially in the Saʿid, that provided for a steady flow of agricultural migrant labor to Lower Egypt, the aristo-crats effectively blocked a full capitalist development in Egypt. Since the upper middle class depended on the aristocrats for venture capital, their fortunes became tied to the aristocracy. This new ruling class worked to create a parliamentary monarchial state that continued to be tied to the British. This was the case because the aristocracy needed the British to repress any moves from the lower classes to remove the aristocracy from their privileged position in Egyptian society. The mutual dependency of the British, the palace, the upper middle class, and the aristocracy served to limit any attempts by the Wafd to liberalize and democratize civil soci-ety in Egypt. Therefore, though the Wafd represented the hopes of all the Egyptian people, it did little to advance the economic and political well-being of the lower classes or to effectively end British colonialism in Egypt.

Ruling-class women's role in the creation and maintenance of their class and the state was complex. By creating a cultural construct of gen-der based on a woman's reproductive and social reproductive capabilities that they worked to reify as the national ideal, these women created a state culture that their class could employ to win consent from lower-class Egyptians. Although spatial separation with blurred spheres existed in the harem tradition, the new Westernized cultural feminist construct acknowledged separate spheres for men and women, even when they occupied the same public space. Elite women created a cultural feminist organization, the Egyptian Feminist Union, and tied it to the international cultural feminist movement. This connection revealed the EFU's affiliation with the West and provided the EFU with international recognition and status. Not all elite women agreed with the feminists on every issue, but they did support the basic premise of cultural feminism: that a woman was simply her nature, a wife and a mother.

Ruling-class women convinced lower-class Egyptians of the reality of their construct through their control of social institutions, extensions of their contribution to *waqf* through which they could create self-regulatory practices among the lower classes. By opening *ouvroirs*, clinics, and schools, the women promoted their agenda to convince all Egyptian females that their citizenship was based on their roles as wives and mothers. If the recipients of their philanthropy failed to marry, their role would be to work as domestic servants or textile workers. Men were to remain the primary producer while women were to become consumers. Elite women's promotion of the Western woman as the model for Egyptian females fueled the lower classes' desire for Western goods, ensuring that lower-class women would have to continue to work in some capacity. Elite women also attempted to create self-regulatory practices among nonelite women and, interestingly, their own men through their attempts at prohibiting smoking, drinking, and prostitution, citing that these activities were unhealthy. Lower-class women were most affected by these attempts as they, and not men of any class, were to be found in the *ouvroirs*, schools, and clinics. Protective legislation for working women, advocated by elite women and working-class men, who thought that it was unhealthy for women to work long hours or in the evening, curtailed working women's ability to work longer hours and to make up lost wages.

Elite women's national construct of woman also impacted professional women by circumscribing the types of professions females could pursue, professions that were outgrowths of the role as wife and mother. As elite women did not have to engage in waged work, they sought to limit lower-class women's access to waged work, though nonelite women could ill afford any reduction in work or pay. Elite women worked from the cultural feminist model that women were the same, employing gender as a category of analysis. What was good for ruling-class women would be equally good for all Egyptian women. What has not yet been analyzed is the extent to which the ruling-class feminists' push for Egyptian women to be wives and mothers first and foremost impacted on increased fertility rates in Egypt. Although the cultural feminist model may have worked for nation-states in the West at this time, the effect on Egypt, with its declining economy, would prove devastating.

Even as they were successful in incorporating cultural feminism into the state culture, elite women fought their marginalization in Islamic law. They wanted to apply the same law to their men, thereby removing them from the influence of secular law. Secular law benefited elite men who saw themselves vis-à-vis their women and the Egyptian lower classes in much the same way that Europeans saw Egyptians as a whole. Ruling-class Egyptian men could claim rights based on positivist and Social Darwinist ideas of their superiority, leaving no rights, only duty and morality, to their women and the lower classes. This marginalization of ruling-class women may explain their initial backing of the Wafd.

When the Wafd failed to incorporate the women's demands into an effective political platform, elite women employed romanticism and challenged their men's secularism with the reformist Islam of Muhammad 'Abduh. Though Social Darwinists, 'Abduh and his disciples employed their *salafism* against ruling-class men's secularism; elite women simply followed suit. By doing so, they could maintain their ties to the West while still attacking their men's secularism with religion. Their social reform activities with respect to ending the use of alcohol and prostitution were intended to clean up public space and to induce self-regulation on the part of the lower classes. As the political situation in Egypt became more divisive in the 1930s, with the collapse of the cotton economy and the rise of the extraparliamentary organizations, elite women turned away from Egypt, involving themselves in the broader international cultural feminist movement and elite Arab women's activities. As pacifists, a quality they believed to be innately female, they could not support armed struggle against the British or the Egyptian state. Did this position mitigate the increasing violence from the lower classes in Egypt toward the state and the British who supported it?

As evidenced in the elite journals, most women of this class did not promote women's direct political participation. Those of the EFU and the organization's journals *L'Egyptienne* and *al-Misriya* did support demonstrations and boycotts but not women's direct involvement in political organizations, whether parliamentary or extraparliamentary. They relied on the vote as a means to affect change in the public sphere from their position in the private sphere, in keeping with the Western cultural feminist position. They sought suffrage for elite women after women had become sufficiently educated. In multiple ways, the elite continued to acknowledge the organic duality of spheres for men and women, a decidedly Western liberal construct. They chose to work from their romanticist, woman's sphere, while their men worked from their liberal, positivist, male sphere. As a result, they were able to secure their position in the new Egyptian state while continuing to battle their men on issues of religion and morality. Since ruling-class women's activities aided their class's hegemony, elite men did not seek to disband the EFU.

Though the elite's creation and employment of social institutions helped reify their construct of woman as the hegemonic state construct, their creation of a discourse of cultural feminism in their published journals also aided this goal. The use of French or Modern Standard Arabic as the medium for the transmission of their construct reflected their connection to the West. They also sought to ground their feminism in more of the Western heritage tradition than that of the Islamicized Egyptian tradition. Hence, their journals focused on women of the Pharaonic period, a time in Egyptian history that the West also claims. The achievements of modern Western women were also highlighted in their journals. Since their discourse centered more on women's issues directly than on broader economic and political issues, their journals were more typical of writing developed by women in the West. It was a feminine genre of writing that was different but complemented men's writing.

Managerial women's relationship to public space and the public sphere differed considerably from that of ruling-class women. Women of this class eagerly entered the professions and managed to obtain a certain degree of status in them without formal training before the creation of professional standards. The professionals mediated ruling-class women's movement from the harem/salon to public space and to the public sphere of discourse, something that did not occur with respect to *salonnière* women in eighteenth-century France (Goodman 1998, 224), who did not possess the same power as women in Egypt. They did not have access to the public sphere while in private space as harem women did. They also had to depend on male professionals, who were less than enthusiastic about helping women promote their agenda in public space and the public sphere. Therefore, the Egyptian historical situation was quite unique.

Professional women acknowledged ruling-class women's activities in the social arena, promoting education for women, the right to divorce, and other reforms. They often called for professional men to include elite women in their activities to a greater degree. They also admired the women's battle with their men over the Muslim personal status law, which reminded the statesmen of their duty to females and to the lower classes. Professional women in Egypt allied with the elite to gain financial assistance and social status for their own projects, including their journals. In turn, managerial women used their professional positions to support elite women's issues. As journalism was linked to other professions, such as the theater and entertainment, professional women in Egypt had broad access to both the public sphere and public space. Therefore, a cross-class alliance of ruling-class and professional women did exist, reflecting a degree of "woman or gender as a category of analysis" model.

Even though a cross-class alliance of women did exist in Egypt reflecting the dominant Women's or Gender Studies paradigm, elite- and professional-class women came into conflict over issues relating to their respective classes. Managerial women's relationship to public space and the public sphere differed considerably from that of the elite. Never having been sexually segregated in the harem, nonelite women always worked in public space, and their private sphere roles as wives and mothers had not yet become as distinct from their public sphere roles as had been the case with harem women. The imposition of women's private sphere into public space created sexual segregation where it did not formerly exist, causing professionals to choose between being a wife and mother or a worker. If they chose the latter, they found that their identity had become tied to their role as wife and mother when they entered production, circumscribing what jobs they could do, when they could do them, and at what pay. The hegemonic construct of woman and the system of sexual segregation also affected lower-class women because their men employed domesticity as a means to keep women at home and out of competition with them in the labor market, especially during the Great Depression. As a result, while ruling-class women employed domesticity to get lower-class women into female production, if the need arose, lower-class men employed domesticity to get their women to stay home.

Professional women who were consenting to the hegemonic construct of woman and discourse of cultural feminism were resisting it at the same time by creating alternative constructs. Resistance came in the form of actively working for a wage or in waged professions. The women identified themselves with their professions and supported those who wanted to work at jobs that were not extensions of their roles as wives and mothers, including entertainment, engineering, journalism, law, newspaper sales, and police work. Fatima al-Yusuf and Munira Thabit supported women working directly in public space. Nabawiya Musa and Labiba Ahmad stressed spatial separation for the two genders while acknowledging that women could access the public sphere from private space.

Similarly, they supported women's economic success and encouraged competition in the economic sphere. Professional women were aggressive; they worked hard, and though some people may have considered them aberrant, they did not share this perspective. They possessed a keener understanding of the dynamics of the family among the lower classes, questioning who would take care of the children. The added pressure of two people working also led lower-class women to consider a family wage for men. Like ruling-class women, managerial women were not always in agreement over the means of deconstructing the hegemonic ideal of woman, only its end. By challenging this aspect of state culture, they acted to subvert the Egyptian state as a whole.

Instead of emphasizing social reform, professional women's primary focus was the achievement of their gender's direct political participation. Although they admired the social work of their elite counterparts, they also understood the effect of social reforms in creating self-regulatory practices. Consequently, they challenged these aspects to send a message to elite women that they would take from them what was beneficial but would refuse aspects of the reforms that were designed to control the lower classes. In this vein, professional women did not blindly accept their roles as wives and mothers in the political and social arena. Just as they had done in the economic arena, they sought to enter politics directly, either through parliamentary or extraparliamentary activities and organizations. Unlike their elite sisters, they did not believe that women had to evolve, or become more educated, to participate directly in politics, nor did they believe that it reduced their womanhood in any way to do so.

Though elite women were anti-imperialist, professional women took their anti-imperialism to a new level. Some women, including Fatima al-Yusuf and Munira Thabit, continued to work within the existing parliamentary system but supported extraparliamentary activities. They also became more ardently anti-imperialist and anti-Western. Both began journals in support of the Wafd but became increasingly anti-Wafdist by the early 1930s. Munira Thabit joined the EFU in an attempt to change the direction of the organization but, like Nabawiya Musa earlier, found that her brand of feminism differed from the cultural feminism of the elite. Both Thabit and al-Yusuf supported the protest activities of the Egyptian youth movement. Other women turned increasingly toward other extraparliamentary activities and organizations.

Ruza Antun Haddad's socialist direction moved further to the left from the socialism she shared earlier with her brother, Farah Antun. Labiba Ahmad, also an early supporter of the Wafd, eventually became associated with the *salafism* of Rashid Rida and Hasan al-Banna, the founder of the Muslim Brotherhood. Her journal became a mouthpiece for the Islamists in the 1930s. Nabawiya Musa, a founding member of the EFU, favored oligarchy and absolutist monarchy over democratic, parliamentary government by the late 1930s. Though she seemed to understand the appeal of fascism, she became disillusioned with the fascist experiments in Europe.

Managerial women's resistance to the Egyptian state and its ruling class was matched by their resistance to the British colonial presence in Egypt and to the West in general. They attacked Western consumerism as a byproduct of elite women's reliance on Western women as models. Ironically, while the institutional feminists called to boycott Western products to encourage indigenous industry, their construct of woman had the effect of encouraging the consumption of Western goods. Managerial women understood that boycotts would not be enough, and they went about dismantling the elite women's reified construct. Instead of opting for alliances with other Arab women and cultural feminists internationally, they sought to make successful Egyptian nationalism a reality. They resisted the culture of the elite and the state by focusing on Egyptian heritage, not from the Pharaonic period, but from the Islamic period in Egyptian history. Part of this heritage orientation included the *salafi* trend of Rashid Rida, who influenced Hasan al-Banna, the founder of the Muslim Brotherhood. Unlike Muhammad 'Abduh, who provided a secularized and Westernized vision for Islam, Rida and al-Banna sought a more authentic Islam devoid of Western influences. Their *salafism* became part of the nationalist, anticolonialist struggle that appealed to the Egyptian managerial class.

Part of their resistance to the West and imperialism involved the language that professional women chose to transmit their ideas. They promoted the use of Arabic alone and decried the Europeanization of the language in the creation of the *fusha*. This standardization of the language paralleled that of the professions in Egypt that adversely affected women's ability to easily access the professions without formal training. Unlike elite women who fought their marginalization under Islamic law, professional women had to fight their own men, who allied with the ruling class in the creation of a standard hegemonic state culture. Professional women's decision to employ Arabic alone, with the incorporation of the *'ammiya,* or the Egyptian vernacular, exemplified their resistance to the West, to the ruling class, and to their own men.

Managerial women, then, attempted to hold on to their niche in the professions in Egypt and to keep the door open to women like themselves. They resisted the hegemonic state culture in two ways: They either attempted to hold on to their place in public space and their access to the public sphere of economics and politics, or they attempted to remain in private space and to dismantle the Western liberal concept of spheres entirely. As the ruling class relied on reified cultural constructs, such as gender and language, to persuade lower-class Egyptians to consent to the ruling class's control of the nation-state, professional women's creation of alternative cultural constructs, reified through their discourse in their journals and through their participation in various activities, acted to subvert the hegemonic constructs and the elite's hegemony. Their conflicts outweighed their alliances, and by the 1930s, the cross-class alliance of women in Egypt began to crack. As a result, cultural feminism and parliamentary politics in Egypt would be in crisis throughout the 1940s. What followed was not only a direct result of their collusion but of their conflict as well.

Glossary

References

Index

Glossary

'amma: general public, masses

'ammiya: popular language usually employed for speaking

Al-Azhar al-Sharif: oldest university in the world that contains a mosque, located in Cairo.

Dar al-Kutub: Egyptian National Library

Dawriyat: periodical section of library

dhikrayat: memoirs

feddan: a unit of land measurement which equals 1.038 acres

fellah; pl. *fellahin:* peasant

fusha: literary Arabic (Modern Standard), usually not spoken but only employed for reading and writing

al-hajja: she who has made her pilgrimage to Mecca

hanim: a title for elite ladies

iltizam: tax farm

khassa: elite

Majlis al-Shuyukh: council of elders, senate

mudhakkirat: memoirs

mujahida: female jihadist

multazima; pl. *multazimat:* female tax farmer

ouvroir: workshop

polyglossia: many languages

purdah: veil

Sa'id: Upper Egypt

salafism (salafiya): Islamic reform movement founded by Muhammad 'Abduh in the nineteenth century.

salonnière: French women who hosted salons for Enlightenment *philosophes* in the eighteenth century

shababist: relating to youth *(shabab)* movement in Egypt in the 1930s

Shari'a: Islamic law

Sirdar: supreme commander of Anglo-Egyptian army

'ulama: community of learned men (religious)

waqf; pl. *awqaf:* an Islamic religious endowment

zajal: popular form of Arabic poetry, written in the *'ammiya*. The form is meant to be improvised on the spot and recited (to music) by two opposing teams who then dialogue with each other.

zar: a popular form of mental healing carried out by women in North Africa. Women of many religions participate in zar.

References

'Abbas, Ra'uf. 1986. *Jama'at al-Nahda al-Qawmiya*. Cairo: Dar al-Fikr.

'Abbas, Ra'uf, and 'Asim Dasuqi. 1998. *Kibar al-Mullak wa al-Fellahin fi Misr 1837–1952*. Cairo: Dar al-Qiba'.

'Abd al-Rahman, Muhammad Sadiq. 1932. "Al-Ittihad al-Nisa'i." *al-Nahda al-Nisa'iya*, no. 5 (May): 145–48.

Abdel Kader, Soha. 1987. *Egyptian Women in a Changing Society, 1899–1987*. Boulder, Colo.: Lynne Rienner.

'Abduh, Ibrahim. 1961. *Ruz al-Yusuf*. Cairo: Mu'assasat Sijill al-'Arab.

———. 1982. *Tatawwur al-Sihafa al-Misriya*. Cairo: Mu'assasat Sijill al-'Arab.

Abou-El-Haj, R. A. 2000. "Historiography in West Asian and North African Studies since Sa'id's *Orientalism*." In *History after the Three Worlds: Post-Eurocentric Historiographies*, ed. Arif Dirlik, Vinay Bahl, and Peter Gran, 67–84. Lanham, Md.: Rowan and Littlefield.

Abu al-Isa'ad, Muhammad. 1994. *Nabawiya Musa wa Dauruha fi al-Haya al-Misriya (1886–1951)*. Cairo: Al-Hay'a al-Misriya al-'Amma li al-Kitab.

Abu Lughod, Lila. 1986. *Veiled Sentiments: Honor and Poetry in a Bedouin Society*. Berkeley: Univ. of California Press.

———. 1993. *Writing Women's Worlds: Bedouin Stories*. Berkeley: Univ. of California Press.

Abu al-Majd, Sabri. 1986. *Muhammad al-Taba'i*. Cairo: Dar al-Ta'awun.

Ahmad, Labiba. 1932. "Ila Mata." *al-Nahda al-Nisa'iya*, no. 9 (Sept.): 289–92.

Ahmed, Leila. 1982. "Feminism and Feminist Movements in the Middle East, A Preliminary Exploration: Egypt, Algeria, People's Democratic Republic of Yemen." In *Women and Islam*, ed. Azizah al-Hibri, 153–68. Oxford: Pergamon Press.

———. 1989. "Arab Culture and Writing Women's Bodies." *Feminist Issues* 9:41–55.

———. 1992. *Women and Gender in Islam: Historical Roots of a Modern Debate.* New Haven: Yale Univ. Press.

Al-Ali, Nadje Sadig. 2000. *Secularism, Gender, and the State in the Middle East: The Egyptian Women's Movement.* Cambridge: Cambridge Univ. Press.

Allen, Roger. 2000. *An Introduction to Arabic Literature.* Cambridge: Cambridge Univ. Press.

al-Amal. 1926. No. 47 (Sept. 25): 4–8.

"Al-Anisa Munira Thabit." 1928. *al-Nahda al-Nisa'iya,* no. 62 (Feb.): 49.

"L'apôtre de la non-violence." 1931. *L'Egyptienne,* no. 75 (Dec.): inset.

Armstrong, Nancy. 1990. "Some Call It Fiction: On the Politics of Domesticity." In *The Other Perspective of Gender and Culture: Rewriting Women and the Symbolic,* ed. Juliet Flower MacCannell, 59–84. New York: Columbia Univ. Press.

Badran, Margot. 1986. *Harem Years: The Memoirs of an Egyptian Feminist.* New York: The Feminist Press.

———. 1988. "Dual Liberation: Feminism and Nationalism in Egypt, 1870–1924." *Feminist Issues* 8:15–34.

———. 1991. "Competing Agenda: Feminists, Islam and the State in Nineteenth- and Twentieth-Century Egypt." In *Women, Islam and the State,* ed. Deniz Kandiyoti, 201–36. Philadelphia: Temple Univ. Press.

———. 1995. *Feminists, Islam and Nation: Gender and the Making of Modern Egypt.* Princeton: Princeton Univ. Press.

"Banatuna wa al-Madaris al-Ajnabiya." 1928. *al-Nahda al-Nisa'iya,* no. 68 (Aug.): 256.

al-Banna, Hasan. 1968. "The New Renaissance." In *Political and Social Thought in the Contemporary Middle East,* ed. Kemal H. Karpat, 115–22. New York: Praeger.

Baraka, Magda. 1998. *The Egyptian Upper Class between Revolutions 1919–1952.* Reading, England: Ithaca Press.

Barakat, 'Ali. 1978. *Milkiya al-Zira'iya bayna Thawratayn 1919–1952.* Cairo: Markaz al-Dirasat al-Siyasiya wa al-Istra'tijiya bi al-Ahram.

Baron, Beth. 1994. *The Women's Awakening in Egypt: Culture, Society, and the Press.* New Haven: Yale Univ. Press.

———. 2005. *Egypt as a Woman: Nationalism, Gender, and Politics.* Berkeley: Univ. of California Press.

Bennholdt-Thomsen, Veronika. 1988. "Why Do Housewives Continue to be Created in the Third World, Too?" In *Women: The Last Colony,* ed. Maria Mies,

Veronika Bennholdt-Thomsen, and Claudia von Werlhof, 159–67. London: Zed Books.

Boddy, Janice. 1989. *Wombs and Alien Spirits: Women, Men, and the Zar Cult in Northern Sudan.* Madison: Univ. of Wisconsin Press.

Booth, Marilyn. 1992. "Colloquial Arabic Poetry, Politics, and the Press in Modern Egypt." *International Journal of Middle East Studies* 24:419–40.

———. 2001. *May Her Likes Be Multiplied: Biography and Gender Politics in Egypt.* Berkeley: Univ. of California Press.

Boserup, Ester. 1970. *Woman's Role in Economic Development.* New York: St. Martin's Press.

Botman, Selma. 1999. *Engendering Citizenship in Egypt: The History and Society of the Modern Middle East.* New York: Columbia Univ. Press.

Brink, Judy H. 1991. "The Effect of Emigration of Husbands on the Status of their Wives: An Egyptian Case." *International Journal of Middle East Studies* 23:201–11.

"Al-Bulis al-Niswi." 1930. *al-Nahda al-Nisa'iya,* no. 88 (Apr.): 110–11.

Butler, Judith. 1990. *Gender Trouble: Feminism and the Subversion of Identity.* London: Routledge.

Charlton, Sue Ellen M., Jana Everett, and Kathleen Staudt. 1989. "Women, the State, and Development." In *Women, the State, and Development,* ed. Sue Ellen M. Charlton, Jana Everett, and Kathleen Staudt, 1–19. Albany: SUNY Press.

Chatterjee, Partha. 1989. "The Nationalist Resolution of the Women's Question." In *Recasting Women: Essays in Indian Colonial History,* ed. Kumkum Sangari and Sudesh Vaid, 223–53. New Brunswick: Rutgers Univ. Press.

Cole, Juan Ricardo. 1981. "Feminism, Class, and Islam in Turn-of-the-Century Egypt." *International Journal of Middle East Studies* 13:387–407.

"Le congrès féministe de Beyrouth." 1930. *L'Egyptienne,* no. 57 (May): 17–19.

Dasuqi, 'Asim. 1981. *Nahwa Fahm Tarikh Misr al-Iqtisadi, al-Ijtima'i.* Cairo: Dar al-Kitab al-Jami'.

Davis, Angela Y. 1983. *Women, Race, and Class.* New York: Random House.

Dawson, Janis. 2003. "Little Women Out to Work: Women and the Marketplace in Louisa May Alcott's *Little Women* and *Work*." *Children's Literature in Education* 34:111–30.

Diamanti, Filio. 2001. "Enemy Sisters: Conflict between Class and Gender Identities in Classical Marxist Feminism, the Cases of Bebel, Zetkin, Kollontai, and Luxemburg." *Studies in Marxism* 8:109–26.

Di-Capua, Yoav. 2004. "'Jabarti of the Twentieth Century': The National Epic of 'Abd al-Rahman al-Rafi'i and Other Egyptian Histories." *International Journal of Middle East Studies* 36:429–50.

Dirlik, Arif. 2000. "Is There History after Eurocentrism? Globalism, Postcolonialism, and the Disavowal of History." In *History after the Three Worlds: Post-Eurocentric Historiographies,* ed. Arif Dirlik, Vinay Bahl, and Peter Gran, 25–47. Lanham, Md.: Rowan and Littlefield.

Donovan, Josephine. 1985. *Feminist Theory: The Intellectual Traditions of American Feminism.* New York: Frederick Ungar.

Les droits de la femme. 1928. No. 3 (Nov. 18): 4–5.

Dussel, Enrique. 1995. "Eurocentrism and Modernity (Introduction to the Frankfurt Lectures)." In *The Postmodernism Debate in Latin America,* ed. John Beverley, Michael Aronna, and José Oviedo, 65–76. Durham: Duke Univ. Press.

Ehrenreich, Barbara. 2001. *Nickel and Dimed: On (Not) Getting by in America.* New York: Metropolitan Books.

Elsadda, Hoda, and Emad Abu-Ghazi. 2001. *Significant Moments in the History of Egyptian Women.* Vol. 1. Cairo: National Council for Women.

"Al-Fallah wa al-Qutn." 1937. *al-Fatah,* no. 2 (Oct. 27): 10.

al-Fatah. 1937. No. 11 (Dec. 30): 15–16.

"Fatah Tajma'u Tharwa Kabira bi Tafkiriha" (Girl Amasses Great Fortune by Her Wits). 1930. *al-Nahda al-Nisa'iya,* no. 86 (Feb.): 54.

Feinberg, Harriet. 1990. "A Pioneering Dutch Feminist Views Egypt: Aletta Jacob's Travel Letters." *Feminist Issues* 10:65–78.

"Femme." 1930. *L'Egyptienne,* no. 54 (Feb.): 4.

Fenoglio-Abd El Aal, Irene. 1988. *Defense et illustration de L'Egyptienne.* Cairo: Centre d'Etudes et de Documentation Economique, Juridique et Sociale.

Fernandes, Leela. 1997. "Beyond Public Spaces and Private Spheres: Gender, Family, and Working-Class Politics." *Feminist Studies* 23:525–47.

Fessenden, Tracy. 2000. "The Convent, the Brothel, and the Protestant Woman's Sphere." *Signs: Journal of Women in Culture and Society* 25:451–78.

Foucault, Michel. 1969. *L'archeologie du savoir.* Paris: Gallimard.

Frevert, Ute. 1989. *Women in German History from Bourgeois Emancipation to Sexual Liberation.* Translated by Stuart McKinnon Evans, Barbara Norden, and Terry Bond. Hamburg: Berg.

Fuda, Hazim. 1972. *Nujum Shari'a al-Sihafa.* Cairo: Akhbar al-Yawm.

Gailey, Christine W., and Thomas C. Patterson, eds. 1987. *Power Relations and State Formation*. Washington, D.C.: American Anthropological Association.

Ganguly-Scrase, Ruchira. 2003. "Paradoxes of Globalization, Liberalization, and Gender Equality: The Worldviews of the Lower Middle Class in West Bengal, India." *Gender and Society* 17:544–66.

Garfield, Seth. 2001. *Indigenous Struggle at the Heart of Brazil: State Policy, Frontier Expansion, and the Xavante Indians, 1937–1988*. Durham: Duke Univ. Press.

Ghoussoub, Mai. 1987. "Feminism—or the Eternal Masculine—in the Arab World." *New Left Review* 161:3–18.

Goodman, Dena. 1998. "Women and the Enlightenment." In *Becoming Visible: Women in European History*, ed. Renate Bridenthal et al., 233–62. 3rd ed. Boston: Houghton Mifflin.

Gramsci, Antonio. 1971. *Selections from the Prison Notebooks*. Translated by Quintin Hoare and Geoffrey Nowell-Smith. New York: International Publishers.

Gran, Judith. 1977. "Impact of the World Market on Egyptian Women." *MERIP Reports*, no. 58:3–7.

Gran, Peter. 1989. "The Virtues of 'Blurring Genres': Merging Political Economy and Islamic Studies to Study Egyptian Culture, the Case of Rights and Obligations." Paper presented at the 23rd conference of the Middle East Studies Association, November, in Toronto, Ontario, Canada.

———. 1996. *Beyond Eurocentrism: A New View of Modern World History*. Syracuse: Syracuse Univ. Press.

Gunther-Canada, Wendy. 2003. "Cultivating Virtue: Catharine Macauley and Mary Wollstonecraft on Civic Education." *Women and Politics* 25:47–71.

Gutmann, Matthew C. 2002. *The Romance of Democracy: Compliant Defiance in Contemporary Mexico*. Berkeley: Univ. of California Press.

Haddad, Ruza. 1927. "Matalib al-Sayidat." *al-Sayidat wa al-Rijal* 3 (Jan.): 173–78.

———. 1929. "al-Sayidat wa al-Mu'tamar wa al-Ma'rid." *al-Sayidat wa al-Rijal* 3 (Jan.): 212–14.

Haeri, Niloofar. 2003. *Sacred Language, Ordinary People: Dilemmas of Culture and Politics in Egypt*. New York: Palgrave Macmillan.

Hammami, Rema, and Martina Rieker. 1988. "Feminist Orientalism and Orientalist Marxism." *New Left Review* 170:93–106.

Hancock, Mary. 2001. "Home Science and the Nationalization of Domesticity in Colonial India." *Modern Asian Studies* 35:871–903.

Harlow, Barbara. 1992. *Barred: Women, Writing, and Political Detention*. Middletown, Conn.: Wesleyan Univ. Press.

Hasanayn, Sa'ad. 1930. "al-Mar'a wa Man' al-Muskirat" (Woman and the Prohibition of Alcohol). *Ummahat al-Mustaqbal,* no. 1 (Jan. 15): 22–23.

Hatem, Mervat. 1986. "The Politics of Sexuality and Gender in Segregated Patriarchal Systems: The Case of Eighteenth- and Nineteenth-Century Egypt." *Feminist Studies* 12:251–74.

———. 1988. "Egypt's Middle Class in Crisis: The Sexual Division of Labor." *Middle East Journal* 42:407–22.

———. 1989a. "Egyptian Upper- and Middle-Class Women's Early Nationalist Discourses on National Liberation and Peace in Palestine (1922–1944)." *Women and Politics* 9:49–69.

———. 1989b. "Through Each Other's Eyes: Egyptian, Levantine-Egyptian, and European Women's Images of Themselves and of Each Other (1862–1920)." *Women's Studies International Forum* 12:183–98.

Hejazi, Yasser. 2006. "The Moment of Awakening: A Hungarian Orientalist Finds Islam." *IslamOnline.net,* April 12, 2006. http://www.islamonline.net/english/Journey/2006/04/jour01.shtml (accessed June 28, 2006).

Herrera, Linda. 2000. "Overlapping Modernities: From Christian Missionary to Muslim Reform Schooling in Egypt." Paper presented at Middle East Institute Conference, Bellagio, Italy, August 2000, http://www.ciaonet.org/conf/mei01/hel01.html (accessed 3/31/2005).

Hodgson, Marshall G. S. 1974. *The Venture of Islam*. Vol. 3. Chicago: Univ. of Chicago Press.

Hoogvelt, Ankie. 1997. *Globalization and the Postcolonial World: The New Political Economy of Development*. 2nd ed. Baltimore: The Johns Hopkins Univ. Press.

Hourani, Albert. 1981. *The Emergence of the Modern Middle East*. Berkeley: Univ. of California Press.

———. 1983. *Arabic Thought in the Liberal Age 1798–1939*. Cambridge: Cambridge Univ. Press.

"Huquq al-Mar'a." 1930. *Ummahat al-Mustaqbal,* no. 1 (Jan. 15): 12–13.

Hussein, Mahmoud. 1973. *Class Conflict in Egypt, 1945–1970*. Translated by Michel and Susanne Chirman, Alfred Ehrenfeld, and Kathy Brown. New York: Monthly Review Press.

Ibrahim, Hassan Ahmed. 1976. *The 1936 Anglo-Egyptian Treaty: An Historical Study with Special Reference to the Contemporary Situations in Egypt and the Sudan*. Khartoum: Khartoum Univ. Press.

Ibrahim, Isma'il. 1997. *Suhufiyat Tha'irat*. Cairo: Dar al-Misriya al-Lubnaniya.

Idris, Yusuf. 1978. "Dregs of the City." *The Cheapest Nights*. London: Heinemann.

Irigaray, Luce. 1993. *Je, Tu, Nous: Toward a Culture of Difference*. New York: Routledge.

Jankowski, James P. 1975. *Egypt's Young Rebels: "Young Egypt," 1933–1952*. Stanford: Hoover Institute Press.

Jayawardena, Kumari. 1986. *Feminism and Nationalism in the Third World*. London: Zed Press.

"La jeune fille et le travail." 1930. *L'Egyptienne*, no. 63 (Nov.): 2–8.

Kabbani, Rana. 1986. *Europe's Myths of Orient*. Bloomington: Indiana Univ. Press.

—————. 1994. *Imperial Fictions*. London: Pandora Press.

Kandiyoti, Deniz A. 1987. "Emancipated but Unliberated? Reflections on the Turkish Case." *Feminist Studies* 13:317–38.

Karam, Azza M. 1998. *Women, Islamisms and the State*. New York: St. Martin's Press.

"Karitha al-Qutn al-'Alamiya wa Kayfa Tu'aliju." 1926. *al-Sayidat wa al-Rijal* 2 (Dec.): 74–78.

Karlsen, Carol F. 1987. *Devil in the Shape of a Woman: Witchcraft in Colonial New England*. New York: Vintage.

"Kayfa Ustuqbila *al-Amal* fi 'Alam al-Suhuf al-Misriya." 1925. *al-Amal*, no. 2 (Nov. 14): 12–13.

"Kayfa Tabgiu al-Sa'ada fi al-Bayt." 1930. *al-Mar'a al-Misriya*, nos. 1, 2 (Feb. 15): 6.

"Kayfa Tafqidu al-Fatah Fursa al-Zawaj." 1930. *al-Mar'a al-Misriya*, nos. 1, 2 (Feb. 15): 4.

Keddie, Nikki R. 1979. "Problems in the Study of Middle Eastern Women." *International Journal of Middle East Studies* 10:225–40.

Khalifa, Ijlal. 1966. "Al-Sihafa al-Nisa'iya fi Misr." Master's thesis, Cairo Univ.

—————. 1973. *Al-Haraka al-Nisa'iya al-Haditha*. Cairo: al-Matba'a al-'Arabiya al-Haditha.

"Khawatir Tha'ira." 1926. *al-Amal*, no. 14 (Feb. 6): 8.

Khoury, Philip. 1984. "Syrian Urban Politics in Transition: The Quarters of Damascus during the French Mandate." *International Journal of Middle East Studies* 16:507–40.

Kicza, John E., ed. 1993. *The Indian in Latin American History: Resistance, Resilience, and Acculturation*. Wilmington, Del.: Scholarly Resources.

Kishtainy, Khalid. 1985. *Arab Political Humour.* London: Quartet Books.

Landau, Jacob M. 1958. *Studies in the Arab Theater and Cinema.* Philadelphia: Univ. of Pennsylvania Press.

Leacock, Eleanor, Helen Safa, et al. 1986. *Women's Work: Development and the Division of Labor by Gender.* New York: Bergin and Garvey.

Le Gassick, Trevor. 1991. "The Gadfly of the Egyptian State." *The World and I* 6, no. 2 (Feb.): 443–45.

MacLeod, Arlene Elowe. 1991. *Accommodating Protest: Working Women, the New Veiling, and Change in Cairo.* New York: Cambridge Univ. Press.

Majaj, Lisa Suhair, Paula W. Sunderman, and Therese Saliba, eds. 2002. *Intersections: Gender, Nation, and Community in Arab Women's Novels.* Syracuse: Syracuse Univ. Press.

Mallon, Florencia E. 2000. "The Promise and Dilemma of Subaltern Studies: Perspectives from Latin American History." In *History after the Three Worlds: Post-Eurocentric Historiographies,* ed. Arif Dirlik, Vinay Bahl, and Peter Gran, 191–220. Lanham, Md.: Rowan and Littlefield.

Malti-Douglas, Fedwa. 1991. *Woman's Body, Woman's World: Gender and Discourse in Arabo-Islamic Writing.* Princeton: Princeton Univ. Press.

"Al-Mar'a al-Misriya wa al-Israf al-Mukharrib." 1926. *al-Amal,* no. 18 (Mar. 6): 8.

"Al-Mar'a fi 'Ahd Fara'ina." 1929. *Fatat al-Sharq* 2 (Nov.): 57–59.

Marcos, Sylvia. 1999. "Twenty-Five Years of Mexican Feminisms." *Women's Studies International Forum* 22:431–33.

Mariscotti, Cathlyn. 1994. "Consent and Resistance: The History of Upper and Middle Class Egyptian Women Reflected through Their Published Journals 1925–1939." Ph.D. diss., Temple Univ.

Marshall, Susan E. 1997. *Splintered Sisterhood: Gender and Class in the Campaign against Women's Suffrage.* Madison: Univ. of Wisconsin Press.

Marsot, Afaf Lutfi al-Sayyid. 1978. "The Revolutionary Gentlewomen in Egypt." In *Women in the Muslim World,* ed. Lois Beck and Nikki R. Keddie, 261–76. Cambridge: Harvard Univ. Press.

Mayers, Marilyn Anne. 1984. "A Century of Psychiatry: The Egyptian Mental Hospitals." Ph.D. diss., Princeton Univ.

Memmi, Albert. 1965. *The Colonizer and the Colonized.* New York: Orion Press. Reprint, Boston: Beacon Press, 1970.

Mernissi, Fatima. 1988. "Muslim Women and Fundamentalism." *Middle East Reports,* no. 153: 8–11.

Michel, Alex. 1928. "Féminisme." *Les droits de la femme,* no. 3 (Nov. 18): 1–3.

Mies, Maria. 1986. *Patriarchy and Accumulation on a World Scale: Women in the International Division of Labor.* London: Zed Books.

Moghadam, Valentine M. 1993. *Modernizing Women: Gender and Social Change in the Middle East.* Boulder, Colo.: Lynne Rienner.

Mohanty, Chandra Talpade, Ann Russo, and Lourdes Torres, eds. 1991. *Third World Women and the Politics of Feminism.* Bloomington: Indiana Univ. Press.

Murad, Mahmud. 1980. *I'tirafat Ihsan 'Abd al-Quddus.* Cairo: al-Matba'a al-'Arabiya al-Haditha.

Musa, Nabawiya. 1937. "Quwa al-Umam fi Ittihadiha." *al-Fatah,* no. 3 (Nov. 3): 4.

"Mushkila Filastin" 1937. *al-Misriya,* no. 11 (July 15): 2–3.

Nabarawi, Ceza. 1930. *L'Egyptienne,* no. 62 (Oct.): 2–17.

———. 1935. "La semaine de la femme." *L'Egyptienne,* no. 110 (Feb.): 3–12.

al-Nadim, 'Abdallah. 1881. "Tahdhib al-Banat min al-Wajibat." *al-Tankit wa al-Tabkit* 9 (Aug. 7): 142–46. Repr. in compilation *al-Tankit wa al-Tabkit,* ed. 'Abd al-Mun'im Jumay'i and 'Abd al-'Azim Ramadan, 176–80. Cairo: al-Hay'a al-Misriya al-'Amma li al-Kitab, 1994.

———. 1994. *Al-A'dad al-Kamila li-Majallat al-Ustaz.* Ed. 'Abd al-Mun'im Jumay'i. Volumes 1 and 2. Cairo: Al-Hay'a al-Misriya al-'Amma li al-Kitab. (Orig. pub. 1892–93.)

"Nahda al-Mar'a fi al-Sharq." 1928. *al-Nahda al- Nisa'iya,* no. 68 (Aug.): 256.

al-Nahda al-Nisa'iya. 1929. No. 73 (Jan.): 1–2.

al-Nahda al-Nisa'iya. 1930. No. 85 (Jan.): 9.

"Nahnu wa Italiya." 1937. *al-Fatah,* no. 4 (Nov. 11): 8.

Navarro, Marysa, and Virginia Sanchez Korrol. 1999. *Women in Latin America and the Caribbean: Restoring Women to History.* Bloomington: Indiana Univ. Press.

Nazim, Mahmud Ramzi. 1931. "Al-Mar'a al-Misriya wa Ummahat al-Mustaqbal." *Ummahat al-Mustaqbal,* no. 19 (Mar. 13): 10–12.

Nazim Bey, 'Abd al-'Aziz. 1937. *L'Egyptienne* (Nov.):6–7.

Nelson, Cynthia. 1986. "The Voices of Doria Shafik: Feminist Consciousness in Egypt, 1940–1960." *Feminist Issues* 6:15–32.

———. 1996. *Doria Shafik, Egyptian Feminist: A Woman Apart.* Gainesville: Univ. Press of Florida.

Olea, Raquel. 1995. "Feminism: Modern or Postmodern?" In *The Postmodernism Debate in Latin America,* ed. John Beverley, Michael Aronna, and José Oviedo, 192–200. Durham: Duke Univ. Press.

Ong, Aihwa. 1988. "Colonialism and Modernity: Feminist Re-presentations of Women." *Inscriptions* 3–4:79–93.

Patterson, Thomas C. 1987. "Tribes, Chiefdoms, and Kingdoms in the Inca Empire." In *Power Relations and State Formation,* ed. Christine W. Gailey and Thomas C. Patterson, 117–25. Washington, D.C.: American Anthropological Association.

Pekacz, Jolanta T. 1997. "Gender as a Political Orientation: Parisian *Salonnières* and the Querelle des Bouffons." *Canadian Journal of History* 32:405–14.

Philipp, Thomas. 1978. "Feminism and Nationalist Politics in Egypt." In *Women in the Muslim World,* ed. Lois Beck and Nikki R. Keddie, 277–94. Cambridge: Harvard Univ. Press.

Posusney, Marsha Pripstein. 1991. "Workers Against the State: Actors, Issues and Outcomes in Egyptian Labor/State Relations." Ph.D. diss., Univ. of Pennsylvania.

Powell, Eve Trout. 2003. *A Different Shade of Colonialism: Egypt, Great Britain and the Mastery of the Sudan.* Berkeley: Univ. of California Press.

Predelli, Line Nyhagen. 2000. "Sexual Control and the Remaking of Gender." *Journal of Women's History* 12:81–104.

"Le prix Nobel de la paix." 1932. *L'Egyptienne,* no. 76 (Jan.): 32.

al-Qaba'ni, 'Abd al-'Alim. 1973. *Nash'a al-Sihafa al-'Arabiya bi al-Iskandariya 1873–1882.* Cairo: al-Hay'a al-Misriya al-'Amma li al-Kitab.

Quijano, Anibal. 1995. "Modernity, Identity, and Utopia in Latin America." In *The Postmodernism Debate in Latin America,* ed. John Beverley, Michael Aronna, and José Oviedo, 201–16. Durham: Duke Univ. Press.

Ramadan, 'Abd al-'Azim Muhammad. 1983. *Tatawwur al-Haraka al-Wataniya fi Misr min 1918 ila 1936.* 2nd ed. Cairo: Maktabat Madbuli.

Reid, Donald Malcolm. 1975. *The Odyssey of Farah Antun: A Syrian Christian's Quest for Secularism.* Minneapolis: Bibliotheca Islamica.

———. 1990. *Cairo University and the Making of Modern Egypt.* Cambridge: Cambridge Univ. Press.

Richard, Nelly. 1995. "Cultural Peripheries: Latin America and Postmodernist De-centering." In *The Postmodernism Debate in Latin America,* ed. John Beverley, Michael Aronna, and José Oviedo, 217–22. Durham: Duke Univ. Press.

Rieker, Martina. 1998. "The Beautification of al-Quds." *Jerusalem Quarterly File* 1:37–42.

al-Risala. 1938. February 7.

Rizk, Dr. Yunan Labib. 2000. "Egyptian Women Make Their Mark." *Al-Ahram: A Diwan of Contemporary Life* 337, no. 481 (May 11–17): 8–17, http://weekly. ahram.org.eg/2000/481/chrncls/htm (accessed June 6, 2005).

———. 2001. "Back Roads." *Al-Ahram: A Diwan of Contemporary Life* 393, no. 537 (June 7–13): 1–7, http://weekly.ahram.org.eg/2001/537/chrncls.htm (accessed June 8, 2005).

———. 2002a. "Women Police." *Al-Ahram: A Diwan of Contemporary Life* 458, no. 602 (Sept. 5–11): 1–6, http://weekly.ahram.org.eg/2002/602/chrncls.htm (accessed June 8, 2005).

———. 2002b. "Gandhi in Egypt." *Al-Ahram: A Diwan of Contemporary Life* 473, no. 617 (Dec. 19–25): 1–5, http://weekly.ahram.org.eg./2002/617/chrn-cls.htm (accessed June 8, 2005).

Rugh, William A. 1979. *The Arab Press.* Syracuse: Syracuse Univ. Press.

Ruz al-Yusuf. 1934. No. 353 (Nov. 26): 17.

Ruz al-Yusuf. 1935. No. 371 (April 1): 35.

Ruz al-Yusuf. 1935. No. 404 (Nov. 18): 6, 36.

Said, Edward W. 1979. *Orientalism.* New York: Vintage Books.

El-Said, Ismail. 1990. *The Communist Movement in Egypt 1920–1988.* Syracuse: Syracuse Univ. Press.

Salamini, Leonardo. 1981. *The Sociology of Political Praxis: An Introduction to Gramsci's Theory.* London: Routledge and Kegan Paul.

Salim, Latifa Muhammad. 1984. *al-Mar'a al-Misriya wa al-Tagyir al-Ijtima'i.* Cairo: al-Hay'a al-Misriya al-'Amma li al-Kitab.

Sanders, Valerie. 1996. *Eve's Renegades: Victorian Anti-Feminist Women Novelists.* New York: St. Martin's Press.

"Al-Sayida Nabawiya Musa wa Wazir al-Ma'arif." 1926. *al-Amal,* no. 18 (Mar. 6): 11.

"Al-Sayidat fi al-Bulis al-Misri." 1930. *Ummahat al-Mustaqbal,* no. 2 (Feb. 15): 110–11.

Selim, Samah. 2004. *The Novel and the Rural Imaginary in Egypt, 1880–1985.* London: Routledge Curzon.

Sha'rawi, Huda. 1929. "Daur al-Mar'a fi Haraka al-Tatawwur al-'Alami." *Fatat al-Sharq,* no. 3 (Dec.): 125–36.

———. 1935. "Les sanglantes consequences d'un discours maladroit." *L'Egyptienne,* no. 117 (Nov.): 2–6.

Sheehi, Stephen. 1999. "Desire for the West, Desire for the Self: National Love and the Colonial Encounter in an Early Arabic Novel." http://social.chass.ncsu.edu/jouvert/v3i3/sheehi htm.

"Shu'un al-Nuzum al-Ijtima'iya." 1928. *al-Sayidat wa al-Rijal*, 2 (Dec.): 74–78.

Sonbol, Amira El-Azhary. 1996. "Adults and Minors in Ottoman *Shari'a* Courts and Modern Law." In *Women, the Family, and Divorce Laws in Islamic History*, ed. Amira El-Azhary Sonbol, 236–56. Syracuse: Syracuse Univ. Press.

———. 2000. *The New Mamluks: Egyptian Society and Modern Feudalism*. Syracuse: Syracuse Univ. Press.

Soto, Shirlene. 1990. *Emergence of the Mexican Woman: Her Participation in Revolution and Struggle for Equality*. Denver: Arden Press.

Spelman, Elizabeth. 1988. *Inessential Women: Problems of Exclusion in Feminist Thought*. Boston: Beacon.

Spivak, Gayatri. 1987. *In Other Worlds: Essays in Cultural Politics*. New York: Methuen.

Stansell, Christine. 1994. "Women, Children, and the Uses of the Streets: Class and Gender Conflict in New York City, 1850–1860." In *Unequal Sisters*, ed. Vicki L. Ruiz and Ellen Carol Dubois, 111–27. 2nd ed. New York: Routledge.

Stern, Steve J. 1995. *The Secret History of Gender: Women, Men, and Power in Late Colonial Mexico*. Chapel Hill: Univ. of North Carolina Press.

al-Subki, Amal Kamil Bayumi. 1986. *Al-Haraka al-Nisa'iya fi Misr ma bayn al-Thawratayn 1919 wa 1952*. Cairo: al-Hay'a al-Misriya al-'Amma li al-Kitab.

Talhami, Ghada. 1996. *The Mobilization of Muslim Women in Egypt*. Gainesville: Univ. Press of Florida.

"Tamasha 'ala al-Ard." 1935. *Ruz al-Yusuf*, no. 372 (Apr. 8): 26.

Tax, Meredith. 1980. *The Rising of Women: Feminist Solidarity and Class Conflict, 1880–1917*. New York: Monthly Review Press.

Thabit, Munira. 1945. *Thawra fi al-Burj al-'Aji*. Cairo: Dar al-Ma'arif.

Tomiche, Nada. 1968. "Egyptian Women in the First Half of the Nineteenth Century." In *Beginnings of Modernization in the Middle East*, ed. William R. Polk and Richard L. Chambers, 171–84. Chicago: Univ. of Chicago Press.

Toth, James. 1991. "Pride, Purdah, or Paychecks: What Maintains the Gender Division of Labor in Rural Egypt?" *International Journal of Middle East Studies* 23:213–36.

Tucker, Judith E. 1979. "Decline of the Family Economy." *Arab Studies Quarterly* 1:245–71.

————. 1985. *Women in Nineteenth-Century Egypt*. Cambridge: Cambridge Univ. Press.

"Al-Ummahat fi Faransa." 1930. *al-Mar'a al-Misriya*, no. 3 (Mar. 15): 47.

Ummahat al-Mustaqbal. 1932. No. 22 (Sept. 1): cover.

Vatikiotis, P. J. 1991. *The History of Egypt from Muhammad Ali to Mubarak*. 4th ed. Baltimore: Johns Hopkins Univ. Press.

Visvanathan, Nalini. 1997. Introduction to Part 1 of *The Women, Gender and Development Reader*. Ed. Nalini Visvanathan et al., 17–32. London: Zed Books.

Vitalis, Robert. 1995. *When Capitalists Collide: Business Conflict and the End of Empire in Egypt*. Berkeley: Univ. of California Press.

von Werlhof, Claudia. 1988. "The Proletariat is Dead: Long Live the Housewife." In *Women: The Last Colony*, ed. Maria Mies, Veronika Bennholdt-Thomsen, and Claudia von Werlhof, 168–81. London: Zed Books.

Walkowitz, Judith R. 1980. *Prostitution and Victorian Society: Women, Class, and the State*. Cambridge: Cambridge Univ. Press.

al-Yusuf, Fatima. 1953. *Dhikrayat*. Cairo: Kitab Ruz al-Yusuf.

Zeidan, Joseph T. *Arab Women Novelists: The Formative Years and Beyond*. Albany: SUNY Press, 1995.

Index

professional-class men (*cont.*)
employment of domesticity, 69–70,
102, 142; insistence on seclusion/
veiling, 58; professional women's
resistance presented by, 132
professional-class women: alliance with
elite women, 25, 26, 39–40, 56–57,
61, 62–63, 75, 85, 87–94, 108–9, 112,
122, 133, 141, 145; alliance with
peasantry, 47, 103–5, 109; alliance
with wage-earning women, 96–103,
109; alternative construct of woman,
40, 101–2, 113, 135, 142, 145; anti-
Western/anti-imperialist sentiments,
112–13, 116, 120–22, 132, 143, 144;
approach to politics, 112–20, 133, 143;
association with extraparliamentary
organizations, 40, 47, 59, 61, 89, 112,
116, 118–20, 123, 133, 143; attempt to
maintain position/collapse separate
spheres, 61, 89, 102; calls for social
justice, 89, 109, 126; challenge to
ruling class's hegemony, 47, 112, 145;
concern for family structure, 101–2,
142; conflict between ruling-class
women and, 27, 88–89, 94–109,
112–33, 141–42, 143; consent to elite's
construct of woman, 35, 50, 89–91,
93–94, 138; consent to ruling-class
women's hegemony, 50, 61, 88, 90–93,
108–9; construct of Egypt/Egyptians,
89; direct challenge to state/cultural
feminism, 39, 40, 58, 59–60, 61, 63,
89, 94, 96–107, 109, 112, 113, 123–24,
126–32, 126–33, 144; direct participation in public sphere, 59, 89, 117–23,
141, 143; disillusionment with parliamentary politics, 116–17; disillusionment with Wafd, 59–60, 116–17,
118–20; effect of housewifization of,

63–68; employment of morality, 89;
impact of institutional feminism
on, 57–58; issues of interest to, 23;
journals of, 23, 89–90, 114 *(see also
specific journal)*; languages used in
journals of, 31, 61, 89, 113, 127, 131;
liberal nationalist movement and,
109, 110; limitations on waged work
for, 138–39; marginalization of,
47, 57–58, 61, 63–68, 86, 112, 124,
141–42; mediation of elite women's
entrance into public space, 88, 141;
militancy/revolutionary activities of,
122–23; neoliberalism and, 28; political role of, 43; position on women
in the workplace, 101–2, 109, 110;
position on women's participation in
public sphere, 115, 116–17, 120–24,
142; pursuit of programs in public
sphere, 97–98, 112; reexamination
of marriage, 105–7; reputations of,
97–98; resistance to dichotomy of
spheres, 94–102, 113–20; resistance
to domestication of public space,
94–102; resistance to elites demands
for self-regulation, 106–8; resistance
to imperialism, 112–13, 116, 120,
121–22, 131, 132, 144; resistance to
national ideal of womanhood, 35, 39,
61, 94–107, 122–24, 142, 144; resistance to Western values, 61, 106–8,
112–13, 132, 144; response to Palestinian problem, 121; role models of,
8n. 10, 100, 113, 124, 126–27; roles of,
88; scholarship on, 8; self-promotion
of, 95; standardization of professions
and, 33, 42–43n. 14, 61, 112, 113, 124,
128–30, 144; subversion of state, 61,
109, 110, 120, 126–33, 142; support of
salafism, 60, 126; support of Wafd, 57,

95, 114, 143; use of Islamic heritage
model, 60, 113, 124, 125, 126, 132,
144; use of term, 25–27; view of pacifism, 89; view of peasantry, 104–5; on
women police, 68–69, 101–2. *See also*
lower-class women; *specific woman
by name*
professions: democratization of, 33;
Egyptianization of, 11; standardization of, 33, 42–43n. 14, 61, 112, 113,
124, 128–30, 144; women's entrance
into, 31
prostitution: as alternative for wage-
earning women, 70; elite men's
response to ban on, 74; elite women's
fight against, 55, 71, 73–74, 75, 76,
106, 106–8, 138, 139; professional
women's view of, 108
public space: conflation with public
spheres in Western thought, 4;
domestication of, 66–75, 87–88; effect
of domestication of on lower classes,
86; elite women's access to, 91; elite
women's control of civil institutions
in, 38, 67–68, 75–76; managerial
women's hold on, 123; marginalization of professional women in, 61;
municipal claim to in Jerusalem, 75n.
12; place of professional women in,
96–99, 109; reification of separate
spheres for men/women in, 47–55,
63–64, 66–68, 87; resistance to
dichotomy of spheres, 94–102, 113–
20; resistance to domestication of,
94–102; resistance to separate spheres
for men/women in, 89; ruling-class
women's entrance into, 25, 48–55,
86, 136–37, 141; ruling-class women's
transformation of, 39, 54–55, 56–57,
63–70, 86, 87, 139; women's access

to as criteria for freedom, 3, 4, 27;
women's access to in nationalist
movement, 17
public sphere: access to for ruling-class
women, 50–51, 83, 91, 140; conflation with public space in Western
thought, 4; denial of women's role in,
50–52, 84; division between private
sphere and, 70, 141; feminization of,
51–54, 55, 86; home as part of, 102;
lower-class women's influence in, 88,
112; male control of, 47–48; marginalization of professional women
in, 61; place of professional women
in, 89, 96–99, 109, 115, 141; professional-class women's advocacy for
participation in, 89, 112; professional
women's activities in, 59, 88, 117–23,
141, 143; professional women's fight
to hold on to place in, 132; resistance
to dichotomy of spheres, 94–102,
113–20; ruling-class women's indirect
involvement in, 40, 51–53, 68, 75–76,
83–84, 86, 87, 137; women's access to
as criteria for freedom, 27, 52

al-Qaba'ni, 'Abd al-'Alim, 128
al-Qalamawy, Suhayr, 8, 94

race/racial discrimination, 10, 35
radical feminism, 27
Reid, Donald Malcolm, 69n. 6, 103n. 13
religion, 9, 15
Revolution of 1935, 119
Richard, Nelly, 29
Rida, Rashid, 57n. 26, 60, 114, 116, 143
Rieker, Martina, 75n. 12
Rifaat, Alifa, 17